# Wis

# Quotations

# For

# Your

# Journey

ORLA
KELLY
PUBLISHING

FIRST PUBLISHED IN IRELAND IN 2021 BY ORLA KELLY
PUBLISHING.

PRINTED IN IRELAND BY PRINTMYBOOK.COM

ISBN:978-1-914225-75-8

This is a compilation of some of Tadhg McCarthy's favourite
quotations from various authors and sources presented under
different themes. Each author and source has been acknowledged
and no claim or ownership is made by Tadhg McCarthy on any of the
quotes listed, other than on his own.

Dedicated to my Father
Thomas McCarthy who
dispensed Wisdom all
throughout his nine decades
of Life

# Contents

# Introduction

Wise quotations can be defined as a group of words from an original author showing experience, knowledge and good judgement. Included in this book are 60 different areas of life that affect us all and as Isaac Disraeli said, "The Wisdom of the Wise, and the experience of the ages, may be preserved by Quotations".

A good book should inform, educate and entertain and the quotations are arranged in a manner to achieve this. Former actress Marlene Dietrich said, "I love quotations because it is a joy to find thoughts that one might have, beautifully expressed with much authority by someone recognised wiser than oneself".

Many of us may remember a phrase or a quotation from an older relative or mentor that we heard when we were younger that made much sense and helped us on our way. I hope you find additional ones in this book.

Quotations can also help us overcome some challenges we meet on our journey and should you find some inspiring, you can make them into your own personal affirmations. Affirmations can enhance our thinking and enrich our lives.

Researching and compiling this book has been a joy, as it has been a journey back through the ages and as Winston Churchill said, "the further back you look, the further forward you can see". Different quotations will resonate at different times of your life, therefore this is a book that can be dipped into now and also at different times in the future.

Enjoy the book and I hope it will assist you on this magical experience called Life.

# ❦ Achievement ❧

Everyone is trying to accomplish something big,
not realising that life is made up of little things.

**Frank A. Clarke**

You have to be odd to be number one.

**Theodor Geisel**

We judge ourselves by what we feel we are capable of doing.
Others judge us by what we have done.

**Henry W. Longfellow**

Who works achieves and who sows reaps.

**Arabian Proverb**

In times of difficulties, we must not lose sight of our achievements.

**Mao Tse-tung**

Think of yourself on the threshold of unparalleled achievement.
A whole clear, glorious life lies before you. Achieve! Achieve!

**Andrew Carnegie**

I have always admired the ability to bite off more than one
can chew and then chew it.

**William De Mille**

They can achieve who believe they can.

**William Dryan**

To win without risk is to triumph without glory.

**Pierce Corneille**

There are no gains without pains.

**Benjamin Franklin**

Success is to be measured not so much by the position that one has reached in life,
rather by the obstacles which have been overcome while trying to achieve.

**Booker T. Washington**

For achievement, try aspiration, inspiration and perspiration.

**Satchel Paige**

There are only two kinds of people who fail:
those who listen to nobody and those who listen to everybody.

**Thomas M. Beshere**

A lot of success in life and business comes from knowing what you really want to avoid:
like an early death or a bad marriage.

**Charles T. Munger**

They are a success who have lived well, laughed often and loved much,
who have gained the respect of intelligent people, and the love of children.
Who have filled their niche and accomplished their task,
who leave the world a better place than they found it.
Whether by an improved poppy, a perfect poem or a rescued soul,
who has never lacked appreciation of earth's beauty or failed to express it,
who looked for the best in others and gave the best they had.

**Robert Louis Stevenson**

There is nothing noble in being superior to others.
The true nobility is in being superior to your previous self.

**Indian Proverb**

Don't be afraid to give up the good to go for the great.

**John D. Rockefeller**

Don't let the fear of failing be greater than the excitement of achieving.

**Robert Kiyosaki**

The achievement of your goal is assured the moment you commit
yourself to it.

**Mack Douglas**

If you're looking for a formula for greatness, the closest we'll ever
get, I think, is this:
consistency driven by a deep love of the work.

**Maria Popova**

Ability will get you to the top, but it takes character to keep you there.

**Abraham Lincoln**

If there is no dull and determined effort, there will be no brilliant
achievement.

**Hsun-Tzu**

Live so enthusiastically, you cannot fail.

**Dorthea Brande**

Victory – a matter of staying power.

**Elbert Hubbard**

# Adversity

One needs difficulties, they are necessary for health.

**Carl Jung**

Adversity has the effect of eliciting talents, which in prosperous circumstances would have lain dormant.

**Horace**

Adversity is the price of progress, don't bring me anything but trouble – good news weakens me.

**Charles F. Kettering**

Every age has its adversity, by solving which, humanity is helped forward.

**Heinrich Heine**

In prosperity our friends know us, in adversity we know our friends.

**J. Churton Collins**

When you are getting kicked from the rear, it means you are in front.

**Bishop Fulton Sheen**

I'll say this for adversity: people seem to be able to stand it, and that's more than I can say for prosperity.

**Kin Hubbard**

There is no education like adversity.

**Benjamin Disraeli**

We must embrace pain and burn it as fuel for our journey.

**Kenji Miyazawa**


Adversity causes some people to break and others to break records.

**William Arthur Ward**


It's easy enough to be pleasant
when everything goes like a song;
but the man worthwhile
is the man who can smile
when everything is going dead wrong.

**Ella Wheeler Wilcox**


I embraced failure, which made me want success all the more.

**Padraig Harrington**


Every path hath a puddle.

**John Ray**


Stumbling is not falling.

**Portuguese Proverb**


Hurt people, hurt people.

**Charles Eads**


Sometimes you win, sometimes you learn.

**John C. Maxwell**

Whoever said anybody has a right to give up?

**Marian Wright Edelman**

When you have exhausted all possibilities, remember this - you haven't.

**Thomas Edison**

I have been through some terrible things in my life, some of which actually happened.

**Mark Twain**

I have learnt more from my mistakes than from my successes.

**Humphrey Davy**

If there is no struggle, there is no progress.

**Frederick Douglas**

Despair ruins some, presumption many.

**Benjamin Franklin**

There is a bit of magic in everything and some loss to even things out.

**Lou Reed**

Adversity is like a strong wind.
It tears away from us all but the things that cannot be torn,
so that we see ourselves as we really are.

**Arthur Golden**

Show me someone who has done something worthwhile and
I will show you someone who has overcome adversity.

**Lou Holtz**

You'll never find a better sparring partner than adversity.

**Golda Meir**

You will have set backs in your life and adversity.
You can be discouraged by it or have courage to get through it and be
better.

**Austin Seferian-Jenkins**

Turning feelings into words can help us process and overcome
adversity.

**Sheryl Sandberg**

Pain makes one think,
thought makes one wise,
wisdom makes life endurable.

**John Patrick**

Take heart. Suffering, when it climbs the highest, lasts but a little
time.

**Aeschylus**

Mistakes are portals of discovery.

**James Joyce**

He who angers you, conquers you.

**Elizabeth Kenny**

# Attitude

Attitude is everything. So pick a good one.

**Wayne Dyer**

The biggest disability in life is a bad attitude.

**Scott Hamilton**

It's your attitude, not your aptitude that determines your altitude.

**Zig Ziglar**

If you don't like something, change it.
If you cannot change it, change your attitude.

**Maya Angelou.**

Nurture your mind with great thoughts, for
you will never go any higher than you think.

**Benjamin Disraeli**

No one can make you feel inferior without your consent.

**Eleanor Roosevelt**

It is the way we react to circumstances that determines our feelings.

**Dale Carnegie**

Things turn out best for people who make the best of the way things
turn out.

**John Wooden**

An individual's greatest enemies are their own apathy and stubbornness.

**Frank Tyger**


Weakness of attitude becomes weakness of character.

**Albert Einstein**


Not in the clamour of the crowded street,
not in the shouts and plaudits of the throng,
but in ourselves, are triumph and defeat.

**Henry Longfellow**


Your problem isn't the problem; it's your attitude about the problem.

**Ann Brashares**


Excellence is not a skill, it is an attitude.

**Ralph Marston**


The mind is not a vessel to be filled, but a fire to be kindled.

**Plutarch**


Two things define you:
your patience when you have nothing,
and your attitude when you have everything.

**George Bernard Shaw**


An optimist is the human personification of spring.

**Susan J. Bissonette**

Attitudes are nothing more than habits of thought.

**John C Maxwell**

The greatest discovery of all time is that a person
can change their future by changing their attitude.

**John Homer Miller**

Always bear in mind that your own resolution
to succeed is more important than any other one thing.

**Abraham Lincoln**

Take the attitude of a student, never be too big to ask questions,
never know too much to learn something new.

**O. G. Mandin**

A bad attitude is like a flat tyre; you cannot go anywhere until you
change it.

**Joyce Meyer**

A happy person is not a person in a certain set of circumstances,
but rather a person with a certain set of attitudes.

**Hugh Downs**

The world is movement, and you cannot be stationary in your attitude
towards something that is moving.

**Heri Cartier-Bresson**

The world only exists in your eyes.
You can make it as big or as small as you want.

**F. Scott Fitzgerald**

# ❧ Awareness ☙

Only a spiritual being has awareness.

**Chick Corea**

What you are aware of you are in control of.

**Anthony de Mello**

Awareness without action is worthless.

**Phil McGraw**

With awareness comes responsibility and choice.

**Amanda Lindhout**

The key to growth is the introduction of higher dimensions
of consciousness into our awareness.

**Lao Tzu**

Let us not look back in anger, nor forward in fear,
but around in awareness.

**James Thurber**

Every human has 4 endowments:
self-awareness, conscience,
independent will and creative imagination.
These give us the ultimate human freedom.
The power to choose, to respond, to change.

**Stephen Covey**

What is necessary to change a person: to change the awareness of
oneself.

**Abraham Maslow**

Awareness is a key ingredient in success.
If you have it, teach it, if you lack it, seek it.

**Michael B. Kitson**

Awareness is all about restoring your freedom to choose what you want,
instead of what your past imposes on you.

**Deepak Chopra**

An awareness of one's mortality can lead you to wake up
and live an authentic and meaningful life.

**Bernie Sigel**

To be aware of a single shortcoming in oneself, is more useful than
to be aware of a thousand in someone else.

**Dalai Lama**

Greed eats brains.

**German Proverb**

Awareness requires living in the here and now, and
not in the elsewhere, the past or the future.

**Eric Berne**

Happiness is your nature.
It is not wrong to desire it.
What is wrong is seeking it outside, when it is inside.

**Ramana Maharshi**

Rather than being your thoughts and emotions, be the awareness behind them.

**Eckhart Tolle**

Being aware is being aware of one's own mind and the games it plays on itself.

**Robin MacNaughton**

When the awareness of what is achievable brushes your life, your journey has begun.

**Lorii Myers**

You have to learn where your weaknesses end and your strengths start, or you will spend your life focusing on all that falls apart.

**Nikki Rowe**

Awareness takes over from thinking. Instead of being in charge of your life, thinking becomes the servant of awareness.

**Eckhart Tolle**

When I discover who I am, I will be free.

**Ralph Ellison**

Remember there is nothing stable in human affairs.
Therefore, avoid elation in prosperity and undue depression in adversity.

**Socrates**

The ego and the self dwell in the same body.
The former eats the sweet and sour fruits of the tree of life,
while the latter looks on in detachment.

**Mundaka Upanishad**

If you are visited by pain, examine your conduct.

**The Talmud**

When you are totally at peace with yourself, nothing can shake you.

**Deepam Chatterjee**

# Belief

Belief is the ignition that gets you off the launching pad.

**Denis Waitley**

They can conquer who believe they can.

**Virgil**

If you think you can, or if you can't, you're right.

**Henry Ford**

Whatever your mind can conceive and believe, the mind can achieve.

**Napoleon Hill**

To accomplish great things, we must not only act,
but also dream, not only plan but also believe.

**Anatole France**

Belief in oneself is one of the most important bricks in building any
successful venture.

**Lydia M. Child**

The only person you are destined to become is the person you decide
to be.

**Ralph Waldo Emerson**

Assertion is not argument; to contradict the statement
of an opponent is not proof that you are correct.

**Samuel Johnson**

I have found that the greatest help in meeting any problem
with decency and self-respect and whatever courage is demanded,
is to know where you yourself stand.
That is, to have in words what you believe and are acting from.

**William Faulkner**

If it is to be, it's up to me.

**E. Wilford Edmar**

We are inclined to believe those who we do not know
because they have never deceived us.

**Samuel Johnson**

Once we believe in ourselves, we can risk curiosity, wonder,
spontaneous delight
or any experience that reveals the human spirit.

**E. E. Cummings**

The outer conditions of a person's life will always be found to reflect
their inner beliefs.

**James Allen**

One person with a belief is equal to ninety-nine who have only
interests.

**John Stuart Hill**

Believe in yourself. Have faith in your abilities.
Without a humble but reasonable confidence in your
own powers, you cannot be successful or happy.

**Norman Vincent Peale**

A man's got to believe in something. I believe I will have another drink.

**W. C. Fields**

There is nothing that can help you understand your own beliefs better than trying to explain them to an inquisitive child.

**Frank Clarke**

Strength does not come from physical capacity. It comes from an indomitable will.

**Mahatma Gandhi**

In the province of the mind, what one believes to be true either is true or becomes true.

**John Lilly**

Belief is not a matter of choice, but conviction.

**Rising Malevolence**

For those who believe, no proof is necessary.
For those who don't believe, no proof is possible.

**Stuart Chase**

Believe in life.

**W. E. B. Du Bois**

Always remember that you are absolutely unique.
Just like everyone else.

**Margaret Mead**

# ❦ Change ❧

I wanted to change the world. But I have found that the only thing one can be sure of changing is oneself.

**Aldous Mead**

If you want to make enemies, try to change something.

**Woodrow Wilson**

Change is not made without inconvenience, even from worse to better.

**Richard Hooker**

Change is inevitable in a progressive country. Change is constant.

**Benjamin Disraeli**

The absurd man is he who never changes.

**Auguste Barthelmy**

The most effective way to cope with change is to help create it.

**L. W. Lynett**

There is nothing in this world constant, but inconstancy.

**Jonathan Swift**

There is nothing wrong with change, if it is in the right direction.

**Winston Churchill**

Change, not habit, is what gets most of us down;
habit is the stabiliser of human society.
Change accounts for its progress.

**William Feather**

Consider how hard it is to change oneself and
you'll understand what little chance you have to change others.

**Arnold Glasow**

A comfort zone is a beautiful place, but nothing grows there.

**Anonymous**

Change is no modern invention.
It is as old as time and as unlikely to disappear.
It has always to be counted on as of the essence of human experience.

**James Rowland Angell**

To reform a man, you must begin with his Grandmother.

**Victor Hugo**

It is not the strongest of the species that survives,
nor the most intelligent;
it is the one most adaptable to change.

**Charles Darwin**

The measure of intelligence is the ability to change.

**Albert Einstein**

The secret of change is to focus all your energy
not on fighting the old, but on building the new.

**Socrates**

One child, one teacher, one pen and one book can change the world.

**Malala Yousafzai**

Change is inevitable, except from a vending machine.

**Robert E. Gallagher**

When we are no longer able to change the situation,
we are challenged to change ourselves.

**Viktor E. Frankl**

If we don't change, we don't grow. If we don't grow, we aren't living.

**Gail Sheehy**

Sometimes it is the smallest decisions that can change your life
forever.

**Keri Russell**

My friends, love is better than anger. Hope is better than fear.
Optimism is better than despair.
So let's be loving, hopeful and optimistic and we'll change the world.

**Jack Layton**

The thing that lies at the foundation of positive change,
 is service to a fellow human being.

**Lech Walesa**

If you do not change direction, you may end up where you are
heading.

**Lao Tzu**

Change the changeable, accept the unchangeable
and remove yourself from the unacceptable.

**Denis Waitley**

Change before you have to.

**Jack Welch**

Instead of changing, evolve, which is change and growth.

**Tadhg McCarthy**

People change and they forget to tell each other.

**Lillian Hellman**

# Character

The dearest to me, are those of best character.

**African Proverb**

Character is a diamond that scratches every other stone.

**Cyrus R. Bartol**

Character is destiny.

**Heraclitus**

The character of a generation is moulded by personal character.

**Brook Foss Westcott**

A good head and a good heart are always a formidable combination.

**Nelson Mandela**

Character development is the great, if not the sole aim of education.

**William O'Shea**

It's only by the hard blows of adverse fortune that character is tooled.

**Arnold Glasow**

Before you are five and twenty you must establish a character that will serve you all your life.

**Lord Collingwood**

Character is simply habit long continued.

**Plutarch**

Fame is a vapour, popularity an accident, riches take wings.
Only one thing endures, and that is character.

**Horce Greeley**


Bad company corrupts good character.

**Menander**


Know thy self.
Don't accept your dog's admiration as conclusive.

**Mayes**


The world is changed by your example, not by your opinion.

**Paulo Coelho**


Our character is what we do when we think no one is looking.

**H. Jackson Brown**


Don't mistake personality for character.

**Wilma Askinas**


I look to a day when people will not be judged by the colour
of their skin, but by the content of their character.

**Martin Luther King Jr.**


Character is formed, not by laws, commands and decrees,
but by quiet influence, unconscious suggestion and personal
guidance.

**Marion L. Burton**

No one knows their true character until they have run out of gas, purchased something on the instalment plan and raised an adolescent.

**Marcelene Cox**

A man's reputation is the opinion people have of him,
his character is what he really is.

**Jack Miner**

The experience of the ages that are past, the hopes of the ages that are yet to come, unite their voices in an appeal to us;
they implore us to think more of the character of our people than of its vast numbers;
to look upon our vast natural resources, not as tempters to ostentation and pride,
but as a means to be converted by the refining alchemy of education, into mental and spiritual treasures and thus give to the world the example of a nation whose wisdom increases with its prosperity and whose virtues are equal to its power.

**Horace Mann**

If we don't invest now in building character in children,
we will surely invest more tomorrow in trying to repair adults.

**Michael Josephson**

Any fool can criticise, condemn and complain,
but it takes character and self-control to be understanding and forgiving.

**Dale Carnegie**

Only what we wrought into our character during life can we take away with us.

**Alexander Humboldt**


What you are is what you have been and what you will be is what you do now.

**Buddha**


Character is the sum total of all our everyday choices.

**Margaret Jensen**


People of character don't allow the environment to dictate their style.

**Lucille Kallen**


Decency is quiet, but it lasts.

**Anonymous**

# Confidence

Skill and confidence are an unconquered army.

**George Herbert**

Have confidence that if you have done a little thing well,
you can do a bigger thing well too.

**Joseph Story**

If you are prepared, then you are able to feel confident.

**Robert J. Ringer**

To grow and know what one is growing towards:
that is the source of all strength and confidence in life.

**James Baillie**

It is not so much our friends' help that helps us, as the confidence of
their help.

**Epicurus**

Confidence doesn't come out of nowhere; it's a result of hours,
days, weeks and years of constant work and dedication.

**Roger Staubach**

Confidence is going after Moby Dick in a rowing boat
and taking the tartar sauce with you.

**Zig Ziglar**

When you have confidence, you can do anything.

**Sloane Stevens**

Confidence is when you believe in yourself and your abilities.
Arrogance is when you think you are better than others.

**Stewart Stafford**


Experience tells you what to do; confidence allows you to do it.

**Stan Smith**


Get more confidence by doing things that excite and frighten you.

**Jessica Williams**


Every day, in every way, I'm getting better.

**Émile Coué**


The world doesn't care about your self-esteem.
The world will expect you to accomplish something before you feel
good about yourself.

**William Gates**


There's a confidence and sense of self that comes with age that I
didn't anticipate.

**Jillian Michaels**


Because one believes in oneself, one doesn't try to convince others;
because one is content with oneself, one doesn't need others'
approval;
because one accepts oneself, the world accepts him or her.

**Lao Tzu**


Self-confidence is the first requisite to great undertakings.

**Samuel Johnson**

Whatever we expect with confidence becomes our own self-fulfilling prophecy.

**Brian Tracy**

If you are insecure, guess what? The rest of the world is too.
Do not overestimate the competition and underestimate yourself.
You are better than you think.

**T. Harv Eker**

The best lightning rod for your own protection is your own spine.

**Ralph Waldo Emerson**

Our deepest fear is not that we are inadequate.
Our deepest fear is we are powerful beyond measure.
It is our light, not our darkness that frightens us.
We ask ourselves, who am I to be brilliant, talented, fabulous?
Actually who are you not to be?
You are a child of God.
Your playing small does not save the world.

**Marianne Williamson**

A huge light bulb moment for me has been noticing that I need both periods of self-confidence and self-doubt to produce my best work.

**Alice Boyes**

Nothing can dim the light that shines from within.

**Maya Angelou**

No one is you and that is your power.

**David Grohl**

# Courage

Courage is resistance to fear, mastery of fear, not absence of fear.

**Mark Twain**

Life shrinks or expands in proportion to one's courage.

**Anais Nin**

Courage conquers all things.

**Ovid**

Success is never final, failure is never fatal. It's courage that counts.

**George F. Tilton**

There is nothing in the world so admired, as an individual who knows how to bear unhappiness with courage.

**Seneca**

Everyone of courage is a person of their word.

**Pierre Corneille**

The only security is courage.

**Francois De La Rochefoucauld**

One person with courage makes a majority.

**Andrew Jackson.**

Courage consists in equality to the problem before us.

**Ralph Waldo Emerson**

True courage is a result of reasoning.
A brave mind is always impregnable.

**Jeremy Collier**

If I was asked to give the single most useful bit of advice for all humanity, it would be this:
Expect trouble as an inevitable part of life.
And when it comes, hold your head high, look at it squarely in the eye and say I will be bigger than you. You cannot defeat me.

**Ann Landers**

Courage is the thing. All goes if courage goes.

**J. M. Barrie**

Only by going to your limit, can you see what's beyond.

**Thomas A. Martin**

People who don't take risks generally make about two big mistakes a year.
People who do take risks generally make about two big mistakes a year.

**Peter F. Drucker**

Courage is fear holding on a minute longer.

**George S. Patton**

Courage is grace under pressure.

**Ernest Hemingway**

Courage is the first of human qualities, which guarantees the others.

**Aristotle**

Either life entails courage or it ceases to be life.

**E. M. Foster**

Creativity requires the courage to let go of certainties.

**Erich Frohm**


Being deeply loved by someone gives you strength;
loving someone deeply gives you courage.

**Lao Tzu**


One who is not courageous enough to take risks will accomplish
nothing in life.

**Muhammad Ali**


Courage is very important. Like a muscle, it is strengthened by use.

**Ruth Gordon**


Don't let the noise of others' opinions drown out your own inner
voice.
And most important, have the courage to follow your heart and
intuition.

**Steve Jobs**


Pain nourishes courage. You cannot be brave
if you've only had wonderful things happen to you.

**Mary Tyler Moore**


Courage doesn't always roar. Sometimes courage is the little voice at
the end of the day that says, "I'll try again tomorrow".

**Mary Anne Radmacher**


Courage is more exhilarating than fear and in the long run, easier.

**Eleanor Roosevelt**

# Decisions

Quick decisions are unsafe decisions.

**Sophocles**

It is not hard to make decisions, when you know what your values are.

**Roy Disney**

Deliberate with caution, but act with decision;
yield with graciousness, or oppose with firmness.

**Charles Hole**

If you can be really good at destroying your own wrong ideas, that is a great gift.

**Charles T. Munger**

In any moment of decision, the best thing to do is the right thing.
The worst thing you can do is nothing.

**Theodore Roosevelt**

When, against one's will, one is high pressured into making a hurried decision, the best answer is always No.
No is more easily changed to Yes, than Yes is changed to No.

**Charles E. Nielson**

When you come to a fork in the road, take it!

**Yogi Berra**

A wise person makes their own decisions; an ignorant person follows public opinion.

**Chinese Proverb**

When faced with a decision, choose the path that feeds the soul.

**Dorothy Mendoza Row**


The H.A.L.T. Method:
Never make a decision when you are hungry, angry,
lonely or tired.

**David Denotaris**


If you would persuade, appeal to interest, not reason.

**Benjamin Franklin**


No trumpets sound when the important decisions in our life are
made.
Destiny is made known silently.

**Agnes DeMille**


The risk of a wrong decision is preferable to the terror of indecision.

**Maimonides**


Once you make a decision, the universe conspires to make it happen.

**Ralph Waldo Emerson**


There is no wrong time to make the right decision.

**Dalton McGuinty**


A good decision is based on knowledge and not on numbers.

**Plato**


Concision in style, precision in thought, decision in life.

**Victor Hugo**

There is no decision that we can make,
that doesn't come with some sort of balance or sacrifice.

**Simon Sinek**


We think, each of us, that we're much more rational than we are.
And we think that we make our decisions because we have good
reasons to make them, even when it's the other way round.
We believe in the reasons, because we've already made the decision.

**Daniel Kahneman**


Nobody's life is ever all balanced.
It's a conscious decision to choose your priorities every day.

**Elizabeth Hasselbeck**


The chief cause of human errors is to be found in prejudices picked
up in childhood.

**René Descartes**


When making a decision of minor importance, I have always found it
advantageous to consider all the pros and cons.
In vital matters, however, such as the choice of a mate or profession,
decisions should come from the unconscious, from somewhere deep
within ourselves.

**Sigmund Freud**


What we spend our time on, is probably the most important decision
we make.

**Raymond Kurzwell**

# Discipline

Discipline is the bridge between goals and accomplishments.

**Jim Rohn**


Discipline means our ability to get ourselves to do things
that we don't want to do.

**Arden Mahlberg**


Through self-discipline comes freedom.

**Aristotle**


If we don't discipline ourselves the world will do it for us.

**William Feather**


Man must be disciplined, for he is by nature raw and wild.

**Immanuel Kant**


One who lives without discipline is exposed to grievous ruin.

**Thomas A. Kempis**


Discipline is the refining fire by which talent becomes ability.

**Roy L. Smith**


A disciplined mind leads to happiness; an undisciplined mind leads to
suffering.

**Dalai Lama**


Success is nothing more than a few simple disciplines, practiced
every day.

**Jim Rohn**

Persistence beats resistance.

**Michael J. Barry**


If I want to be great, I have to win the victory over myself.....
self-discipline.

**Harry S. Truman**


Without self-discipline, success is impossible, period.

**Lou Holtz**


Mental toughness is many things and rather difficult to explain.
Its qualities are sacrifice and self-denial.
It is combined with a perfectly disciplined Will that refuses to give in.
It is a state of mind called character in action.

**Vince Lombardi**


Moderation is the key to lasting enjoyment.

**Hosea Ballou**


Rules are for the obedience of fools and the guidance of wise people.

**David Ogilvy**


The more disciplined you become, the easier life gets.

**Steve Paulina**


We don't have to be smarter than the rest. We have to be more
disciplined than the rest.

**Warren Buffett**


Success is measured by your discipline and inner peace.

**Michael Ditka**

Motivation gets you going, discipline keeps you growing.

**John C. Maxwell**

Talent without discipline is like an octopus on roller skates.

**H. Jackson Brown**

Self-discipline is the magic power that makes you virtually unstoppable.

**Daniel Kennedy**

Mastering others is strength; mastering yourself is true power.

**Lao Tzu**

Self-discipline is an act of cultivation.
It requires you to connect today's actions to tomorrow's results.
There's a season for sowing, a season for reaping.
Self-discipline helps you know which is which.

**Gary Ryan Blair**

No horse gets anywhere until it is harnessed.
No steam or gas ever drives anything until it is confined.
No Niagara is ever turned into light and power until it is tunnelled.
No life ever grows great until it is focused, dedicated, disciplined.

**Harry Emerson Fosdick**

The most we can get out of life is its discipline for ourselves
and its usefulness for others.

**Tryon Edwards**

Discipline is your friend, not your enemy.

**Joyce Meyer**

# ⤴ Education ⤵

The chief objective of education should be to widen the windows through which we view the world.

**Arnold Glasow**

Education is the ability to listen to almost anything without losing your temper or self-confidence.

**Robert Frost**

The two basic processes of education are, knowing and valuing.

**Robert J. Havighurst**

The aim of a great education is not knowledge but action.

**Herbert Spencer**

Education is no longer thought of as a preparation for adult life, but as a continuing process of growth and development from birth to death.

**Stephen Mitchell**

My idea of education is to unsettle the mind of the young and inflame their intellects.

**Robert Maynard Hutchins**

I had six honest serving men; they taught me all I know. Their names were: where, what, when, why, how and who.

**Rudyard Kipling**

Develop a passion for learning. If you do, you will never cease to grow.

**Anthony J. D'Angelo**

If you think education is expensive, try ignorance.

**Derek Curtis Bok**

Education's purpose is to replace an empty mind with an open one.

**Malcolm S. Forbes**

Tell me and I'll forget,
show me and I may remember,
involve me and I will learn.

**Benjamin Franklin**

Teachers open the door, but you must enter yourself.

**Chinese Proverb**

Where there are 2 PhD's in a developing country,
one is head of state and the other is in exile.

**Lord Samuel**

One pound of learning requires ten pounds of common sense to apply it.

**Persian Proverb**

Try to learn something about everything and everything about something.

**T. H. Huxley**

Ignorance leads to fear, fear leads to hate and hate leads to violence. This is the equation.

**Averroes**

You cannot teach a person anything, you can only help them find it within themselves.

**Galileo Galilei**

No matter how busy you may think you are, you must find time for reading or surrender yourself to self-chosen ignorance.

**Confucius**

Education is the chief defence of nations.

**Edmund Burke**

A professor is one who talks in someone else's sleep.

**W.M. Auden**

The student who graduates today and stops learning tomorrow is uneducated the day after.

**Newton D. Baker**

A teacher affects eternity; one can never tell where their influence stops.

**Henry Adams**

I told my Father I was punished in school because I didn't know where the Azores were.
He told me to remember where I put things in future.

**Henry Youngman**

Only the educated are free.

**Epictetus**

One looks back with appreciation to the brilliant teachers,
but with gratitude to those who touch our human feelings.
The curriculum is so much necessary raw material, but
warmth is the vital element for the growing plant and for
the soul of a child.

**Carl Jung**

Any book which is all important should be reread immediately.

**Charles T. Munger**

Never memorise what you can look up in books.

**Albert Einstein**

Reading without reflecting, is like eating without digesting.

**Edmund Burke**

It must be the aim of education to teach the citizens
that they must first of all rule themselves.

**Winthrop Aldrich**

The person who doesn't read has no advantage over the person who
cannot read.

**Mark Twain**

I am indebted to my father for living, but to my teacher for living well.

**Alexander The Great**

One cannot leave a better legacy to the world than a well-educated
family.

**Thomas Scott**

# Enthusiasm

Enthusiasm is the greatest asset in the world.
It beats money, power and influence.
It is no more than faith in action.

**Henry Chester**

Nothing is so contagious as enthusiasm.

**Edward Bulwer-Lytton**

Enthusiasm is at the bottom of all progress.
With it there is accomplishment.
Without it there are only alibis.

**Henry Ford**

The world belongs to the enthusiast who keeps cool.

**William McFee**

Nothing great was ever achieved without enthusiasm.

**Samuel Taylor Coleridge**

Live so enthusiastically that you cannot fail.

**Dorthea Brande**

In the realm of ideas, everything depends on enthusiasm.
In the real world, all rests on perseverance.

**Johann Wolfgang Von Goethe**

Enthusiasm is not contrary to reason, it is reason on fire.

**Peter Marshall**

The worst bankrupt in the world is the man who has lost his enthusiasm.
Let a man lose everything else in the world, but his enthusiasm and he will come through again to success.

**H. W. Arnold**

Enthusiasts soon understand each other.

**Washington Irving**

Experience and enthusiasm are two fine attributes seldom found in one individual.

**William Feather**

If you aren't fired with enthusiasm, you will be fired with enthusiasm.

**Vince Lombardi**

Probably nothing in the world arouses more false hopes than the first four hours of a diet.

**Samuel Beckett**

The essential in this time of moral poverty is to create enthusiasm.

**Pablo Picasso**

Creativity is a natural extension of our enthusiasm.

**Earl Nightingale**

If you have enthusiasm, you have a very dynamic companion to travel with you on the road to somewhere.

**Loretta Young**

If you have zest and enthusiasm – you attract zest and enthusiasm.
Life does give back in kind.

**Norman Vincent Peale**

Above all, it's important to be optimistic and enthusiastic
when developing ourselves and those around us.

**Richard Hill**

Your interests, desires and abilities are energised by whatever fans
your flame.
Wisdom, energy and enthusiasm – deliver your destiny.

**Mark D. Gleason**

If you can give your children only one gift, let it be enthusiasm.

**Bruce Barton**

Hang on to your youthful enthusiasm; you'll be able to use them
better when you're older.

**Seneca**

Enthusiasm is the electricity of life. How do you get it?
You act enthusiastic until you make it a habit.

**Gordon Parks**

# ❧ Facts ❧

Let us keep our mouths shut and our pens dry until we know the facts.

**A. J. Carlson**

Facts do not cease to exist because they are ignored.

**Aldous Huxley**

Everyone has a right to their opinion, but no one has a right to be wrong in their facts.

**Bernard M. Baruch**

We should keep so close to the facts that we never have to remember what we said the first time.

**F. Marion Smith**

Digging for facts is a better mental exercise than jumping to conclusions.

**Thomas Huxley**

A sure way to stop a red-hot argument is to lay a few cold facts on it.

**Vern McLellan**

Facts when combined with ideas, constitute the greatest force in the world.

**Carl W. Ackerman**

There is nothing more deceptive than an obvious fact.

**Arthur Conan Doyle**

Facts are stubborn things, but statistics are pliable.

**Mark Twain**

Facts don't care about your feelings.

**Ben Shapiro**

Facts are facts and will not disappear on account of your likes.

**Jawaharlal Nehru**

Facts? What are facts? I only know imagination.

**C. Joybll**

Comments are free, but facts are sacred.

**C. P. Scott**

If you believe only in facts and forget stories,
your brain will live, but your heart will die.

**Cassandra Clare**

I'm more interested in arousing enthusiasm in kids than in teaching
the facts.
The facts may change, but that enthusiasm for exploring the world
will remain with them the rest of their lives.

**Seymour Simon**

If you are purely after facts, please buy yourself a phone directory of
Manhattan.
It has 4 million correct facts, but it doesn't illuminate.

**Werner Herzog**

The way to do research is to attack the facts at the point of greatest astonishment.

**Celia Green**


Facts may be coloured by the personalities of the people who present them.

**Reginald Rose**


The fact that a great many people believe something
 is no guarantee of its truth.

**W. Somerset Maughan**


Truth and facts are woven together.
However, sometimes facts can blind you from seeing what is actually going on in someone's life.

**Shannon L. Alder**


The facts are always less than what really happened.

**Nadine Gordimer**


The fact is, we need help and we need each other.

**Kris Carr**

# Family

The Family is one of nature's masterpieces.

**George Santayana**

Nobody's family can hang out the sign, "nothing the matter here".

**Chinese Proverb**

Good family life is never an accident, but always an achievement by those who share it.

**James H. S. Bossard**

Other things may change us, but we start and end with the family.

**Anthony Brandt**

Family, where life begins and love never ends.

**Amy Rees Anderson**

Call it a clan, call it a network, call it a tribe, call it a family; whatever you call it, whoever you are, you need one.

**Jane Howard**

Family, a unit composed not only of children, but of men, women, an occasional animal and the common cold.

**Ogden Nash**

Twenty thousand years ago, the family was the social unit. Now the social unit has become the world, in which it may truthfully be said that each person's welfare affects that of every other.

**Arthur H. Compton**

Families are about love overcoming emotional torture.

**Matt Groening**

Some families can trace their ancestry back over 300 years,
but can't tell you where the children were last night.

**Vern McLellan**

Every family tree produces some nuts.

**Elise Braem**

I have learnt that having a child fall asleep in your arms,
is one of the most peaceful feelings in the world.

**Andrew Rooney**

To maintain a joyful family requires much from both the parents and
the children.
Each member of the family has to become, in a special way, the
servant of the others.

**Pope John Paul II**

Families are the compass that guides us.
They are the inspiration to reach great heights, and our comfort
when we occasionally falter.

**Brad Henry**

Children are one third of our population and all of our future.
**Panel for Promotion of Child Health**

In every conceivable manner, the family is the link to our past and
the bridge to our future.

**Alex Haley**

No matter what you've done for yourself or humanity,
if you can't look back on having given love and attention to your own
family, what have you really accomplished?

**Elbert Hubbard**


Everyone needs a house to live in, but a supportive family is what
builds a home.

**Anthony Liccione**


I sustain myself with the love of family.

**Maya Angelou**


If you plan for a year, plant rice.
If you plan for a decade, plant trees.
If you plan for a century, educate your children.

**Chinese Proverb**


The 3 most important phases in all relationships are:
"Thank you", "I'm sorry" and "I love you".

**Cicely Saunders**


A dysfunctional family is a family with more than one person in it.

**Mary Karr**


What can you do to promote world peace?
Go home and love your family.

**Mother Teresa**

# ❧ Friends ❧

What is a friend? A single soul dwelling in two bodies.

**Aristotle**

A friend is a sheltering tree.

**Samuel Taylor Coleridge**

A friend is one of the nicest things you can have and one of the nicest things you can be.

**Douglas Pagels**

If you make friends with yourself, you will never be alone.

**Maxwell Maltz**

Few delights can equal the mere presence of someone we utterly trust.

**George McDonald**

Don't walk in front of me, I may not follow.
Don't walk behind me, I may not lead.
Just walk beside me and be my friend.

**Albert Camus**

A friend is one who sees through you and still enjoys the view.

**Wilma Askinas**

A friend is a person before whom I may speak aloud.

**Ralph Waldo Emerson**

Good friends are like shock absorbers.
They help you take the lumps and bumps on the road of life.

**Frank Tyger**


I have friends in overalls whose friendship I would not swap
for the favour of the kings of the world.

**Thomas A. Edison**


The language of friendship is not words, but meanings.

**Henry David Thoreau**


Probably the most neglected friend you have is you.

**L. Ron Bubbard**


Some people go to priests, others to poetry; I, to my friends.

**Virginia Woolf**


In everyone's life, at some time, our inner fire goes out.
It is then burst into flame by an encounter with another human
being.
We should all be thankful for those people who rekindle the inner spirit.

**Alber Schweitzer**


Prosperity makes friends, adversity tries them.

**Publilus Syrus**


I don't need a friend who changes when I change and who nods
when I nod; my shadow does that much better.

**Plutarch**

Do not do unto others as you would, that they should do unto you.
Their tastes may not be the same.

**George Bernard Shaw**

The best things in life are never rationed.
Friendship, loyalty, love do not need coupons.

**George T. Hewitt**

I will destroy my enemies by converting them to friends.

**Maimonides**

If a man does not make new acquaintances as he advances through life, he will soon find himself alone.
A Man, Sir, should keep his friendship in constant repair.

**Samuel Johnson**

When the character of someone is not clear to you, look at their friends.

**Japanese Proverb**

Try to be a rainbow in someone's cloud.

**Maya Angelou**

True friends are never apart. Maybe in distance, but never in heart.

**Helen Keller**

There can be no friendship without confidence, and no confidence without integrity.

**Samual Johnson**

If two friends ask you to be judge in a dispute, don't accept because you will lose one friend.
On the other hand, if two strangers come with the same request, accept, because you will gain one friend.

**St. Augustine**

True friendship is like sound health.
The value of it is seldom known until it is lost.

**Charles C. Colton**

# Giving

No one has ever become poor by giving.

**Ann Frank**

Give to the world the best you have and the rest will come
back to you.

**Ella Wheeler Wilcox**

Those who give have all things; those who withhold have nothing.

**Hindu Proverb**

The giving is the hardest part; what does it cost to add a smile.

**Jean De La Bruyere**

No person was ever honoured for what they received.
Honour has been the reward for what they gave.

**Clive Coolidge**

A man there was, and they called him mad;
the more he gave, the more he had.

**John Bunyan**

We make a living by what we get; we make a life by what we give.

**Winston Churchill**

The Lord loveth a cheerful giver. He also accepteth from a grouch.

**Catherine Hall**

There is a wonderful mythical law of nature that the three things we crave most in life –
happiness, freedom and peace of mind – are always attained by giving them to someone else.

**Payton Conway March**


Blessed are those who can give without remembering and take without forgetting.

**Elizabeth Bibesco**


Charity should begin at home, but it should not stay there.

**Philip Brooks**


Remember the poor, it costs nothing.

**Josh Billings**


What I have, I gave,
what I had, I spent,
what I left, I lost by not giving.

**On Christoper Chapman's Headstone**


You have not lived until you have done something for someone who can never repay you.

**John Bunyan**


A small gift is better than a big promise.

**German Proverb**


Service to others is the rent you pay for your room here on earth.

**Mohammed Ali**

If you want something, give it.

**Deepak Chopra**

If nature has made you as a giver, your hands are born open, and so
is your heart;
and though there may be times when your hands are empty, your
heart is always full.

**Frances Hodgson Burnett**

The most truly generous persons are those
who give silently without hope of praise or reward.

**Carol Ryrie Brink**

Giving is not just about making a donation; it is about making a
difference.

**Kath Calvin**

No one is useless in this world who lightens the burdens of another.

**Charles Dickens**

Don't judge each day by the harvest you reap, but by the seeds you
plant.

**Robert Louis Stevenson**

Live simply so that others can simply live.

**Mahatma Gandhi**

# ⤳ Goals ⤳

The most important thing about goals is having one.

**Geoffrey F. Abert**

A person without a purpose is like a ship without a rudder.

**Thomas Carlyle**

The big thing is that you know what you want.

**Earl Nightingale**

Until input (thought) is linked to a goal (purpose), there
can be no intelligent accomplishment.

**Paul C. Thomas**

The poor person is not they without a cent, but they without a dream.

**Harry Kemp**

Obstacles are those frightful things you see when you take your eyes
off your goal.

**Hannah More**

To live only for some future goal is shallow.
It's the sides of the mountain that sustain life, not the top.

**Robert M. Pirig**

You must have long range goals to keep you from being frustrated
from short term failures.

**Charles C. Noble**

A goal is a dream with a deadline.

**Napoleon Hill**


Not failure, but low aim is a crime.

**Ernst Holmes**


My ancestors wandered in the wilderness for 40 years because
in biblical terms, men would not stop to ask for directions.

**Elayne Boosler**


Your direction is more important than speed.

**Richard L. Evans**


Write down on paper your goal in life.
With that down in black and white, we can really get somewhere.
Few can define their goal, much less write it.
You cannot find happiness until your goal is clear and in view.

**Ross Byron**


There are two things to aim at in life:
first, to get what you want, and after that to enjoy it.
Only the wisest of mankind achieve the second.

**Logan Pearsall Smith**


Not doing more than the average is what keeps the average down.

**William Winans**


If you are bored with life and you don't get up every morning with a
burning desire to do things, you don't have enough goals.

**Lou Holtz**

Where so ever you go, go with all your heart.

**Confucius**


Help others to achieve their dreams and you will achieve yours.

**Les Brown**


Three men were laying brick. They were each asked what they were doing.

The first man answered:     Laying some brick
The second man answered:    Earning 5 dollars a day
The third man answered:     I am helping to build a great cathedral
Which person are you?

**Charles M. Schwab**


Discover what you want most of all in this world and set yourself to work on it.

**John Homer Miller**


If you want to be happy, set a goal that commands your thoughts, liberates your energy and inspires your hopes.

**Andrew Carnegie**


You have to set goals that are almost out of reach.
If you set a goal that is attainable without much work or thought,
you are stuck with something below your true talent and potential.

**Stephen Garvey**


Everyone has their own Mount Everest they were put on this earth to climb.

**Seth Godin**

The measure of a society is not only what it does, but the quality of its aspirations.

**Wade Davis**

You are never too old to set another goal or to dream a new dream.

**C. S. Lewis**

Dream! Dream! And then go for it.

**Archbishop Desmond Tutu**

Write your obituary, then write your goals.

**Brigitte Ganger**

Few if any forces in human affairs are as powerful as a shared vision.

**Susan Scott**

The inspiration you seek is already within you.
Be silent and listen.

**Rumi**

# Government

What is the best form of government?
That which teaches us to govern ourselves.

**John Wolfgang Von Goethe**

Government is a trust, and the officers of government are trustees; and both the trust and the trustees are created for the benefit of the people.

**Henry Clay**

You can only govern people by serving them. The rule is without exception.

**Victor Cousin**

Let the people know the truth and the country is safe.

**Abraham Lincoln**

The world has forgotten, in its concern for right and left, that there is an above and below.

**Galen Drake**

A government that robs Peter to pay Paul can always depend on the support of Paul.

**George Bernard Shaw**

The object of government in peace and in war is not the glory of Rulers or of Races, but the happiness of the common man.

**William Beveridge**

Under capitalism man exploits man; under socialism the reverse is true.

**Polish Proverb**

There is no such thing as public opinion, only published opinion.

**Winston Churchill**

Fear is the foundation of most governments.

**John Adams**

The measure of a country's greatness is its ability to retain compassion in times of crisis.

**Thurgood Marshall**

A good newspaper is a nation talking to itself.

**Arthur Miller**

Millions of individuals making their own decisions in the market place will always allocate resources better than any centralised government planning process.

**Ronald Reagan**

Democracy is the theory that the common people know what they want and deserve to get it good and hard.

**H. L. Mencken**

There is far more danger in public than in private monopoly,
for when government goes into business, it can always
shift its losses to the taxpayers.
Government never makes ends meet – and that is the
first requisite of business.

**Thomas A. Edison**

One fifth of the people are against everything all the time.

**Robert Kennedy**

Politics is a jungle; torn between doing the right thing and staying in office.

**John F. Kennedy**

A Politician thinks of the next election; a Statesman thinks of the next generation.

**J. F. Clarke**

It is the duty of Civil Servants to think all around a subject and give Ministers their unbiased opinions...... and then, when policy has been decided on, to carry out that policy to the best of their ability regardless of their personal opinion.

**T. K. Whitaker**

Never do anything against your conscience, even if the State demands it.

**Albert Einstein**

Where the press is free and everyone able to read, all is safe.

**Thomas Jefferson**

He that would govern others, first should be the master of himself.

**Philip Massinger**

My definition of a free society, is a society where it is safe to be unpopular.

**Adlai Stevenson**

I think the worst thing in public life is to not recognise your mistakes.

**T. K. Whitaker**

The 8 stages of democracy are: slavery, spiritual faith, great courage, liberty, abundance, complacency, apathy and dependence.

**Alexander Fraser Tytler**


Great nations write their autobiography in three manuscripts:
the book of their deeds,
the book of their words and
the book of their art.

**John Ruskin**


Nations have no permanent friends or allies.
They only have permanent interests.

**Lord Palmerston**


What are you doing to improve your country?

**David Rubenstein**

# ✺ Gratitude ✺

Enjoy the little things, for one day you may look back and realise they were the big things.

**Robert Brault**

Acknowledging the good you already have in your life is the foundation for all abundance.

**Eckhart Tolle**

Gratitude is a currency that we can mint for ourselves and spend without the fear of bankruptcy.

**Fred De Witt Van Amburg**

You cannot be grateful and fearful at the same time.

**Daniel Baker**

He is a wise man who does not grieve for the things which he has not, but rejoices for those which he has.

**Epictetus**

This is a wonderful day. I've never seen this one before.

**Maya Angelou**

Gratitude is not only the greatest of virtues, but the parent of all others.

**Cicero**

A person may be ungrateful, but the human race is not so.

**John Milton**

As bread is the staff of life, the simple sustenance of the body,
so appreciation is the food of the soul.

**Princilla Wayne**


If you lost everything you had and got it back again, how grateful
would you feel?

**Bertrand Russell**


There is a calmness to a life lived in gratitude, a quiet joy.

**Ralph H. Blum**


Gratitude is a powerful catalyst for happiness.
It's the spark that lights a fire of joy in your soul.

**Amy Collette**


The soul that gives thanks can find comfort in everything;
the soul that complains can find comfort in nothing.

**Hannah Whitall Smith**


Learn to be grateful for what you have, while you pursue all that you
want.

**Jim Rohn**


When it comes to life, the critical thing is whether you take things for
granted or take them with gratitude.

**G. K. Chesterton**


Gratitude and attitude are not challenges, they are choices.

**Robert Braathe**

The struggle ends when gratitude begins.

**Neale Donald Walsh**

I was complaining that I had no shoes,
until on the street, I met a man with no feet.

**Confucius**

Appreciation is a wonderful thing; it makes what is excellent in others
belong to us as well.

**Voltaire**

Gratitude turns what we have into enough.

**Aesop**

There's always something to be thankful for:
if you can't pay your bills, you can be thankful you're not one of your
creditors.

**Anonymous**

Start each day with a positive thought and a grateful heart.

**Roy T. Bennett**

The most beautiful moments in life are moments when
you are expressing your joy, not when you are seeking it.

**Jaggi Vasudev**

If the only prayer you said in your whole life was "Thank You", that
would be enough.

**Meister Eckehart**

# ❧ Happiness ❧

Happiness is but a name,
make content and ease thy aim.

**Robert Burns**


The three grand essentials of happiness:
someone to love, something to do and something to look forward to.

**Alexander Chalmers**


Ask yourself are you happy, and you cease to be.

**John Stuart Mill**


What can be added to the happiness of one who is:
in health, out of debt and has a clear conscience.

**Adam Smith**


Happiness?
That's nothing more than good health and a poor memory.

**Albert Schweitzer**


The secret of happiness is freedom. The secret of freedom is courage.

**Thucydides**


If you want to be happy, be.

**Leo Tolstoy**


Happiness is when what you think, what you say and what you do are
in harmony.

**Mahatma Gandhi**

Thousands of candles can be lit from a single candle,
and the life of the candle will not be shortened.
Happiness never decreases by being shared.

**Buddha**

The greatest happiness you can have is knowing that
you do not necessarily require happiness.

**William Saroyan**

Happiness is not a goal; it's a by-product of a life well lived.

**Eleanor Roosevelt**

Live, and be happy, and make others so.

**Mary Shelley**

A contented mind is the greatest blessing one can enjoy in this world.

**Joseph Addison**

To be without some of the things you want, is an indispensable part
of happiness.

**Bertrand Russell**

Satisfaction of one's curiosity is one of the greatest sources of
happiness in life.

**Linus Pauling**

If I could drop dead now, I'd be the happiest man alive!

**Samuel Goldwyn**

For peace of mind, resign as General Manager of the Universe.

**Larry Eisenberg**

We act as though comfort and luxury were the chief requirements of life, when all that we need to make us happy is something to be enthusiastic about.

**Charles Kinsley**

Tension is who you think you should be. Relaxation is who you are.

**Chinese Proverb**

Don't cry because it's over, smile because it happened.

**Theodor Geisel**

Do not set aside your happiness. Do not wait to be happy in the future. The best time to be happy is always now.

**Roy T. Bennett**

Unhappiness is best defined as the difference between our talents and our expectations.

**Edward de Bono**

We have no more right to consume happiness without producing it, than to consume wealth without producing it.

**George Bernard Shaw**

Enjoy your own life without comparing it with that of another.

**Marquis de Condorcet**

# Health

The six best doctors in the world are:
Rest, Exercise, Diet, Sunshine, Friends and Self-respect.

**Charlie Chaplin**

Sometimes the most urgent and vital thing you can do is take a complete rest.

**Ashleigh Brilliant**

To lengthen thy life, lessen thy meals.

**Benjamin Franklin**

Giving is the secret of a healthy life. Not necessarily money, but whatever one had to give of encouragement, sympathy and understanding.

**John D. Rockefeller**

The people who live long are those who long to live.
As for me, except for an occasional heart attack, I feel as young as I ever did.

**Robert Benchley**

Fear less, hope more; eat less, chew more;
whine less, breathe more; talk less, say more;
hate less, love more; and all good things will be yours.

**Swedish Proverb**

One who has health has hope and one who has hope has everything.

**Thomas Carlyle**

The poorest person would not part with health for money,
but the richest would gladly part with all their money for health.

**C. C. Colton**


Cheerfulness and contentment are great beautifiers
and are famous preservers of youthful looks.

**Charles Dickens**


Never hurry, take plenty of exercise, always be cheerful,
take all the sleep you can get and you may expect to be well.

**J. F. Clarke**


It is part of the cure to wish to be cured.

**Seneca**


If you look like your passport photo, you are too ill to travel!

**Anonymous**


The sovereign invigorator of the body is exercise,
and of all the exercises, walking is the best.

**Thomas Jefferson**


True enjoyment comes from activity of the mind
and exercise of the body; the two are united.

**Alexander Von Humboldt**


Mental health problems do not affect three or four out of every five
persons, but one out of one.

**Dr. Karl Menninger**

To keep the body in good health is a duty, otherwise we shall not be able to keep the mind strong and clear.

**Buddha**

Every negative belief weakens the partnership between mind and body.

**Deepak Chopra**

I have chosen to be happy because it is good for my health.

**Voltaire**

Take care of your body. It's the only place you have to live.

**Jim Rohn**

Those who think they have no time for healthy eating, will sooner or later have to find time for illness.

**Edward Stanley**

Addiction is the number one disease in our civilisation.

**Deepak Chopra**

I believe that the greatest gift you can give your family and the world is a healthy you.

**Joyce Meyer**

# History

History is the version of events that people have decided to agree upon.

**Napoleon Bonaparte**

History is written by the winners.

**George Orwell**

To be ignorant of what happened before you were born is to be ever a child.

**Cicero**

That people do not learn very much from the lessons of history, is the most important of all lessons that history has to teach.

**Aldous Huxley**

History is a vast early warning system.

**Norman Cousins**

Those who do not learn from history are doomed to repeat it.

**George Santayana**

When I want to understand what is happening today or try to decide what will happen tomorrow, I look back.

**Omar Khayyam**

History .... is indeed, little more than the register of the crimes, follies and misfortunes of mankind.

**Edward Gibbon**

It is a fair summary of history to say that the safeguards of liberty
have been forged in controversies involving not very nice people.

**Felix Frankfurter**

Clinging to the past is the problem, embracing change is the answer.

**Gloria Steinem**

History gets thicker as it approaches recent times.

**A. J. P. Taylor**

Tradition means handing on all that is of value to the
next generation.

**Henry Lewis Bullen**

A historian is a prophet in reverse.

**Friedrich Von Schlegel**

The people who have really made history are the martyrs.

**Aleister Crowley**

If you think you have it tough, read history books.

**William Maher**

What do you think has been the effect of the French Revolution?
It is too soon to tell.

**Chairman Mao, 1970**

History is a race between education and catastrophe.

**H. G. Wells**

Two things we ought to learn from history:
one, that we are not in ourselves superior to our fathers;
another, that we are shamefully and monstrously
inferior to them, if we do not advance beyond them.

**Thomas Arnold**


History is who we are, and why we are the way we are.

**David McCullough**


A small body of determined spirits fired by an unquenchable faith in
their mission can alter the course of history.

**Mahatma Gandhi**


Never doubt that you can change history - you already have.

**Marge Piercy**


Study the past, if you divine the future.

**Confucius**


Few of us will ever have the greatness to bend history itself, but each of us
can work to change a small portion of events, and in the total of all
these acts, will be written the history of this generation.

**Robert Kennedy**


Who has fully realised that history is not contained in thick books,
but lives in our very blood.

**Carl Jung**

# ⤙ Honesty ⤚

Honesty plus love will get you through most situations.

**Naval Ravikant**

No legacy is so rich as honesty.

**William Shakespeare**

Honesty: the ability to resist small temptations.

**John Ciardi**

Hard workers are unusually honest; industry lifts them above temptation.

**Christine Bovee**

We look for 3 things when we hire people:
We look for intelligence, energy and integrity;
if you don't get the latter, the other two will kill you.

**Warren Buffett**

Sooner or later, everyone sits down to a banquet of consequences.

**Robert Louis Stevenson**

There is no right way to do something wrong.

**Charles Jewett**

One who has committed a mistake and doesn't correct it, is committing another mistake.

**Confucius**

Good character, like good soup is made at home.

**Amish Proverb**

Let unswerving honesty ever be your watch word.

**Bernard Baruch**

Being honest may not get you a lot of friends but it'll always get you the right ones.

**John Lennon**

Honesty is telling the truth to ourselves and others. Integrity is living the truth.

**Kenneth H. Blanchard**

The real source of inner joy is to remain truthful and honest.

**Dalai Lama**

A lie has speed, but truth has endurance.

**Edgar J. Mohn**

Never be afraid to raise your voice for honesty, truth and compassion against lying and greed.
If people all over the world would do this, it would change the earth.

**William Faulkner**

If you tell the truth, you don't have to remember anything.

**Mark Twain**

I wouldn't believe him if he swore he was lying.

**Milton Berle**

There's just some magic in truth and honesty and openness.

**Frank Ocean**

I think track records are very important.
If you start early trying to have a perfect one in some simple thing like honesty, you're well on your way to success in this world.

**Charles T. Munger**

Honesty is not only the first step towards greatness – it is greatness itself.

**Christian Bovee**

# Humility

Humility is the surest sign of strength.

**Thomas Merton**

There is no need to show off when you know who you are.

**Maxime Lagace**

There is something in humility which strangely exalts the heart.

**St. Augustine**

Stay humble or you'll stumble.

**Dwight L. Moody**

To be humble to superiors is duty, to equals courtesy,
to inferiors nobility.

**Benjamin Franklin**

I believe the first test of a truly great person is their humility.

**John Ruskin**

Humility is attentive patience.

**Simone Weil**

Humility is the mother of giants.
One sees great things from the valley, only small things from the
peak.

**G. K. Chesterton**

Humility is a strange thing; the moment you think you have it,
you have lost it.

**E. D. Hulse**

Humility is the most difficult of all virtues to achieve;
nothing dies harder than the desire to think well of self.

**T. S. Eliot**

Wise people possess humility.
They know that their small island of knowledge is surrounded by a
vast sea of the unknown.

**Harold C Chase**

Life is a long lesson in humility.

**James M. Barrie**

The meek shall inherit the earth, but not its mineral rights!

**J. Paul Getty**

Mastery begins with humility.

**Robin Sharma**

The biggest challenge after success, is shutting up about it.

**Criss Jami**

Never look down on anybody unless you're helping them up.

**Jesse Jackson**

Humility is that low, sweet root, from which all heavenly virtues shoot.

**Thomas Moore**

If you are humble nothing will touch you, neither praise nor disgrace, because you know who you are.

**Mother Teresa**

Pride is the problem, humility is the answer.

**Joyce Mayer**

There is nothing noble in being superior to your fellow man.
True nobility is being superior to your former self.

**Ernest Hemingway**

A true genius admits that they know nothing.

**Albert Einstein**

There is beauty and humility in imperfection.

**Guillermo del Toro**

Humility is not thinking less of yourself, but thinking of yourself less.

**C. S. Lewis**

Every person you meet knows something you don't; learn from them.

**H. Jackson Brown Jr.**

# Humour

Humour is to life, what shock absorbers are to automobiles.

**Barbara Johnson**

Laughter is the tranquilliser with no side effects.

**Arnold Glasow**

Laughter is part of the human survival kit.

**David Nathan**

He who laughs, LASTS.

**Mary Pettibone Poole**

Humour is by far the most significant activity of the human brain.

**Edward De Bono**

Good humour is one of the best articles of dress one can wear in society.

**William M. Thackeray**

Good humour is a tonic for the mind and body.
It is the antidote for anxiety and depression.
It is a business asset.
It attracts and keeps friends.
It lightens human burdens.
It is the direct route to serenity and contentment.

**Grenville Kleiser**

A joke is a very serious thing.

**Charles Churchill**

Humour is emotional chaos remembered in tranquillity.

**James Thurber**


Advice is sometimes transmitted more successfully through a joke
than grave teaching.

**Baltasar Gracián**


A laugh is a pound out of the doctor's pocket.

**Thomas C. McCarthy**


Humour is something that thrives between man's aspirations and his
limitations.
There is more logic in humour than in anything else. Because you
see, humour is truth.

**Victor Borge**


I was married by a Judge. I should have asked for a Jury.

**Groucho Marx**


That's the Irish people all over – they treat a joke as a serious thing
and a serious thing as a joke.

**Sean O'Casey**


Without humour, you cannot run a sweet shop, let alone a nation.

**John Buchan**


A well-developed sense of humour is the pole that adds balance to
your steps as you walk the tightrope of life.

**William Arthur Ward**

There is no life without humour.
It can make the wonderful moments of life truly glorious
and it can make tragic moments bearable.

**Rufus Wainwright**

One of my great regrets and I don't have many, is that I spent too
long putting people's status and reputation ahead of their more
important qualities.
I learnt far too late in life that a long list of letters after someone's
name is no guarantee of compassion, kindness, humour, all the far
more relevant stuff.

**William Nighy**

Laughter is the closest distance between two people.

**Victor Borge**

Humour is the sunshine of the mind.

**Edward G. Bulwer-Lytton**

The most wasted day of all is that on which we have not laughed.

**Nicolas de Chamfort**

He who laughs at himself never runs out of things to laugh at.

**Epictetus**

Laughter is the music of the soul.

**Hap Hagood**

Laughter is the sun that drives winter from the human face.

**Victor Hugo**

# Ideas

There are no hard times for good ideas.

**H. Gordon Selfridge**

Human history is, in essence a history of ideas.

**H. G. Wells**

Ideas come from space.

**Thomas Edison**

A mind that is stretched to a new idea never returns to its original dimension.

**Oliver Wendell Holmes**

Great minds discuss ideas, average minds discuss events, small minds discuss people.

**Eleanor Roosevelt**

A healthy hunger for a great idea is the beauty and blessedness of life.

**Jean Ingelow**

Money never starts an idea; it is the idea that starts the money.

**W. J. Cameron**

To get your ideas across, use small words, big ideas and short sentences.

**John Henry Patterson**

Innovation comes from collaboration.

**William Gates**

Imagination is more important than knowledge.

**Albert Einstein**

Ideas won't keep; something must be done about them.

**Alfred North Whitehead**

Not to engage in the pursuit of ideas is to live like ants instead of people.

**Mortimer Adler**

Getting an idea should be like sitting down on a pin;
it should make you jump up and do something.

**E. L. Simpson**

The power of an idea can be measured by the degree of resistance it attracts.

**David Yoho**

I had a monumental idea this morning, but I didn't like it.

**Samuel Goldwyn**

A good idea for a business:
What problem do I have that no company is providing the solution for?

**Tadhg McCarthy**

There is one thing stronger than all the armies in the world,
and that is an idea whose time has come.

**Victor Hugo**

Ideas are easy.
It's the execution of the idea that really separates the sheep from the goats.

**Susan Grafton**

I value people who have a broad education and experience,
and who have the mind to explore new ideas.

**T. K. Whitaker**

The reason ideas die quickly in some heads is because they can't
stand solitary confinement.

**Herbert V. Prochnow**

If you have an apple and I have an apple and we exchange these
apples, then you and I will still each have one apple.
But if you have an idea and I have an idea and we exchange these
ideas,
then each of us will have two ideas.

**George Bernard Shaw**

Creative thinking inspires ideas. Ideas inspire change.

**Barbara Januszkiewicz**

Story telling is the most powerful way to put ideas into the world
today.

**Robert McAfee Brown**

Wealth flows from ideas and energy.

**William Feather**

Ideas pull the trigger, but instinct loads the gun.

**Don Marquis**

If I have a thousand ideas and only one turns out good, I am satisfied.

**Alfred Nobel**

Take a simple idea and take it seriously.

**Charles Warren**

Curiosity is the key to creativity.

**Akio Morita**

Ideas are a capital that bears interest only in the hands of talent.

**Antoine De Rivrol**

Many ideas grow better when transplanted into another mind
than in the one where they sprung up.

**Oliver Wendell Holms**

# Intelligence

The levels of intelligence are:
smart, intelligent, brilliant, genius, simple.

**Albert Einstein**

Respond intelligently even to unintelligent treatment.

**Lao Tzu**

An intellectual is someone whose mind watches itself.

**Albert Camus**

Intelligence is not to make any mistakes, but to see quickly how to make them good.

**Bertolt Brecht**

Almost everyone is intelligent. It is the method they lack.

**F. W. Nichol**

In order to acquire intellect, one must need it.
One loses it when it is no longer necessary.

**Friedrich W. Nietzsche**

If you would take, you must first give; this is the beginning of intelligence.

**Tao-Te-King**

Intelligence is the effort to do the best you can at your particular job; the quality that gives dignity to that job, whether that happens to be scrubbing a floor or running a corporation.

**J. C. Penney**

When you hire people smarter than you are, you prove you are smarter than they are.

**R. H. Grant**

A moment's insight is sometimes worth a life's experience.

**Oliver W. Holmes**

There are in fact two things, science and opinion;
the former begets knowledge, the latter ignorance.

**Hippocrates**

It is not enough to have a good mind - the thing is to use it well.

**Descartes**

A man is not necessarily intelligent because he has plenty of ideas.
Any more than he is a good general because he has plenty of soldiers.

**Nicolas Chamfort**

Curiosity is one of the permanent and certain characteristics of a vigorous intellect.

**Samuel Johnson**

Genius is 1% inspiration, 99% perspiration.

**Thomas Edison**

Intelligence is not all that important in the exercise of power, and is often, in point of fact, useless.

**Henry Kissinger**

An intelligent person often talks with their eyes,
a shallow person often swallows with their ears.

**Chinese Proverb**


It takes something more than intelligence to act intelligently.

**Fyodor Dostoyevsky**


The ability to observe without evaluating is the highest form of intelligence.

**Jiddu Krishnamurti**


Intelligence without ambition is a bird without wings.

**Walter E. Cottingham**


Be less curious about people and more curious about ideas.

**Marie Curie**


Imagination is only intelligence having fun.

**George Scialabbe**


Failure is simply the opportunity to begin again, this time more intelligently.

**Henry Ford**


The sign of an intelligent person is their ability to control their emotions by the application of reason.

**Marya Mannes**


I'm no genius. I'm smart in spots and I stay around those spots.

**Thomas Watson**

Sometimes the questions are complicated and the answers are simple.

**Theodor Geisel**

If we encounter someone of rare intellect, we should ask them what books they read.

**Ralph Waldo Emerson**

# Investing

The best investment you can make is in yourself.

**Warren Buffett**

Investing is simple, but not easy.

**Warren Buffett**

Compound interest, is the eighth wonder of the world.
One who understands it, earns it, one who doesn't, pays it.

**Albert Einstein**

For young people, invest a regular amount in a tax deferred account
and over time it will amount to something.

**Charles T. Munger**

The four most dangerous words in investing are,
"this time is different".

**John Templeton**

Investing is an activity of forecasting the yield over the lifetime of an
asset.
Speculation is an activity of forecasting the psychology of the market.

**John Maynard Keynes**

In investing, diversification is the only free lunch.

**Harry Markowitz**

Invest based on your psychological makeup, objectives and interests.

**Tadhg McCarthy**

There are two types of forecasters:
those who don't know and those who don't know they don't know.

**Howard Marks**


Being aware of trends and cycles are critical for investing.

**John R. Punch**


Two rules of investing:

Rule Number 1       : Don't lose money

Rule Number 2       : Remember rule number 1.

**Warren Buffett**


Investing is unpredictable so that one has to have different scenarios.

**George Soros**


Capital goes where it is welcome and stays where it is well treated.

**Walter B. Wriston**


There are two times in a man's life when he shouldn't speculate:
when he can't afford it and when he can.

**Mark Twain**


Bull markets are born on pessimism, grow on skepticism,
mature on optimism and die on euphoria.

**John Templeton**


The only function of economic forecasting is to make astrology look respectable.

**John K. Galbraith**

The worst investments are made in the best of times when our guard is down.

**David McWilliams**

The investor's chief problem and even his worst enemy, is likely to be oneself.

**Benjamin Graham**

With each investment we get richer or wiser, never both.

**Mark Yusko**

Investing should be like watching paint dry or watching grass grow. If you want excitement, take $800 and go to Las Vegas.

**Paul Samuelson**

Investing money is the process of committing resources in a strategic way to accomplish a specific objective.

**Alan Gottardt**

Capital can do nothing without brains to direct it.

**J. Ogden Armour**

It is insane to risk what you have and need in order to obtain what you don't need.

**Warren Buffett**

It's one of the most important things, being able to say no to an investment.

**Henry Kravis**

Without numerical fluency, in the part of life most of us inhabit,
you are like a one-legged man in an ass-kicking contest.

**Charles T. Munger**

Risk is when you do not know what you are doing.

**Warren Buffett**

Everyone has the brain power to make money in the stock market,
not everyone has the stomach.

**Peter Lynch**

Earn as much as you can, save as much as you can,
invest as much as you can, give as much as you can.

**John Wesley**

Those who have knowledge don't predict;
those who predict don't have knowledge.

**Lao Tzu**

Buy not on optimism, but arithmetic.

**Benjamin Graham**

# Justice

The welfare of the people is the highest law.

**Cicero**

If we do not maintain justice, justice will not maintain us.

**Francis Bacon**

Justice is the great interest of man on earth.
It is a ligament which holds civilised beings and civilised nations together.

**Daniel Webster**

Justice: a commodity which in a more or less adulterated condition the state sells to its citizens,
as a reward for their allegiance, taxes and personal services.

**Ambrose Bierce**

Justice delayed is justice denied.

**William Gladstone**

If we are to keep our democracy, there must be one commandment: thou shalt not ration justice.

**Learned Hand**

Justice is the insurance we have on our lives and obedience is the premium we pay for it.

**William Penn**

Someone has tabulated we have 35 million laws on the books to enforce the Ten Commandments.

**Bert Masterson**

Discourage litigation. Persuade your neighbour to compromise whenever you can.
As a peacemaker, the lawyer has the opportunity of being a good person. There will still be enough business.

**Abraham Lincoln**

Judging from the main portions of history of the world so far, justice is always in jeopardy.

**Walt Whitman**

Men fight for freedom:
then they begin to accumulate laws to take it away from themselves.

**Thomas Jefferson**

Where law ends, tyranny begins.

**William Pitt**

Justice and judgement lie often a world apart.

**Emmeline Pankhurst**

An eye for an eye only ends up making the whole world blind.

**Mahatma Gandhi**

Laws, like houses lean on one another.

**Edmund Burke**

How much easier it is to be generous than just.
Men are sometimes bountiful who are not honest.

**Junius**

In England, justice is open to all like the Ritz Hotel.

**Sir James Matthew**

Ethics and equity, and the principles of justice do not change with the calendar.

**D. H. Lawrence**

It is certain, in any case, that ignorance allied with power,
is the most ferocious enemy justice can have.

**James Baldwin**

Man's capacity for justice makes democracy possible,
but man's inclination for injustice makes democracy necessary.

**Reinhold Niebuhr**

The criminal justice system, like any system designed by human beings, clearly has its flaws.

**Ben Whishaw**

If you want peace, work for justice.

**Pope Paul II**

There is a higher court than courts of justice and that is the court of conscience.
It supersedes all other courts.

**Mahatma Gandhi**

# Kindness

Be kind, for everyone you meet is fighting a hard battle.

**Plato**

My true religion is kindness.

**Dalai Lama**

The highest wisdom is loving kindness.

**The Talmud**

Three things in human life are important:
The first is to be kind, the second is to be kind and the third is to be kind.

**William James**

Kindness is the oil that takes the friction out of life.

**Seneca**

Kindness is the one commodity of which you should spend more than you earn.

**T. N. Tiemeyer**

I had rather never receive a kindness than never bestow one.

**Seneca**

Kindness is a language the dumb can speak and the deaf can hear and understand.

**Christian Nestell Bovee**

What do we live for, if it is not to make life less difficult for each other?

**George Eliot**

One kind word can warm three winter months.

**Japanese Proverb**

Kindness, in words creates confidence,
in thinking creates profoundness, in giving creates love.

**Lao Tzu**

Choose being kind over being right and you will be right
every time.

**Richard Carlson**

Look back and be grateful, look ahead and be hopeful, and look
around and be helpful.

**Anonymous**

I've learnt that people will forget what you said, people will forget
what you did,
but people will never forget how you made them feel.

**Maya Angelou**

Be kind to unkind people, they need it the most.

**Ashleigh Brilliant**

You can get much further with a kind word and a gun,
than you can with a kind word alone!

**Al Capone**

A kind heart is a fountain of gladness, making everything in its vicinity freshen into smiles.

**Washington Irving**

Hatred and anger are powerless when met with kindness.

**Malcolm X**

Kindness pays most, when you don't do it for pay.

**John Goetsch**

Sometimes it takes only one act of kindness and caring to change a person's life.

**Jackie Chan**

Remember there is no such thing as a small act of kindness.
Every act creates a ripple with no logical end.

**Scott Adams**

Unexpected kindness is the most powerful, least costly
and most underrated agent of human change.

**Robert Kerrey**

Constant kindness can accomplish much.
As the sun makes ice melt, kindness causes misunderstanding,
mistrust and hostility to evaporate.

**Albert Schweitzer**

When I was young, I admired clever people.
Now that I am old, I admire kind people.

**Abraham Joshua Meschel**

If you want to lift yourself up, lift someone else up.

**Booker T. Washington**

The simple act of caring is heroic.

**Edward Albert**

One can pay back the loan of gold, but one dies forever in debt to those who are kind.

**Malay Proverb**

# Leadership

Leadership is the capacity to translate vision into reality.

**Warren G. Bennis**

Leaders are managers of meaning.

**John C. Maxwell**

A leader is a dealer in hope.

**Napoleon Bonaparte**

Real leaders are ordinary people with extraordinary determinations.

**John Seaman Garns**

A great leader never sets themself above their followers, except in carrying responsibilities.

**Jules Ormont**

A leader keeps their fears to themselves, but shares their courage with others.

**Robert Louis Stevenson**

A boss creates fear, a leader confidence;
A boss fixes blame, a leader fixes mistakes;
A boss knows all, a leader asks questions;
A boss makes work drudgery, a leader makes it interesting;
A boss is interested in himself or herself, a leader is interested in the group.

**Russell H. Ewing**

I start with the premise that the function of leadership is to produce more leaders, not more followers.

**Ralph Nader**

Reason and judgement are the qualities of a leader.

**Tacitus**

A leader identifies and polishes ability in people that they didn't realise they had.

**Warren Buffett**

The best leaders almost without exception and at every level, are master users of stories and symbols.

**Tom Peters**

The quality of a leader is reflected in the standards they set for themselves.

**Ray Kroc**

The supreme quality of leadership is unquestionably integrity.

**Dwight D. Eisenhower**

You hire the best people you can possibly find.
Then it's up to you to create an environment where
great people decide to stay and invest their time.

**Rich Lesser**

As a political leader, you start at your least capable and most popular.
You end at your most capable and least popular.

**Tony Blair**

When the best leader's work is done, the people say, "we did it ourselves".

**Lao Tzu**

Leadership is an action, not a position.

**Donald McGannon**

Don't tell people how to do things, tell them what to do and let them surprise you with their results.

**George Patton**

Management is doing things right; leadership is doing the right things.

**Peter F. Drucker**

Leaders must be close enough to relate to others, but far enough ahead to motivate them.

**John C. Maxwell**

A leader is like a shepherd.
He stays behind the flock, letting the most nimble go out ahead, whereupon the others follow, not realising that all along they are being directed from behind.

**Nelson Mandela**

I never thought in terms of being a leader. I thought, very simply of helping people.

**John Hume**

Average leaders raise the bar on themselves, good leaders raise the bar for others, great leaders inspire others to raise their own bar.

**Orrin Woodward**

Before you are a leader, success is all about growing yourself.
When you become a leader, success is all about growing others.

**Jack Welch**

A great leader takes people where they would never go on their own.

**Hans Finzel**

# Leisure

There is no wisdom without leisure.

**Sirach**

Time you enjoy wasting is not wasted time.

**Marthe Troly-Curtin**

What is this life if, full of care, we have not time to stand and stare?

**W. H. Davies**

There is never enough time to do all the nothing you want.

**Bill Watterson**

All intellectual improvement arises from leisure.

**Samuel Johnson**

If you can spend a perfectly useless afternoon in a perfectly useless manner, you have learned how to live.

**Lin Yutang**

The time to relax is when you don't have time for it.

**Sydney J. Harris**

He that will make good use of any part of his life, must allow a large part of it to recreation.

**John Locke**

People who cannot find time for recreation, are obliged sooner or later to find time for illness.

**John Wanamaker**

Each person deserves a day away in which, no problems are confronted, no solutions searched for.

**Maya Angelou**


The world is a book and those who do not travel, read only one page.

**St. Augustine**


Take rest: a field that has rested gives a bountiful crop.

**Ovid**


Fun is like life insurance: the older you get, the more it costs.

**Kin Hubbard**


The supreme accomplishment is to blur the line between work and play.

**Arnold Toynbee**


Every now and then go away, have a little relaxation,
for when you come back to your work your judgement will be surer,
since to remain constantly at work will cause you to lose power of judgement.

**Leonardo Da Vinci**


Leisure is the mother of philosophy.

**Thomas Hobbs**


There is no pleasure in having nothing to do;
the fun is having lots to do and not doing it.

**John W. Raper**

In our leisure, we reveal what kind of people we are.

**Ovid**

The end of labour is to gain leisure.

**Aristotle**

Those who decide to use leisure as a means of mental development,
who love good music, good books, good pictures,
good plays, good company, good conversation –
what are they?
They are the happiest people in the world.

**William Lyon Phelps**

If you are losing your leisure, look out: you may be losing your soul.

**Logan Pearsall Smith**

What we do during our working hours determines what we have;
what we do in our leisure hours, determines what we are.

**George Eastman**

To be able to fill leisure intelligently is the last product of civilisation.

**Bertrand Russell**

Time in nature is not leisure time;
it's an essential investment in our children's health and in our own.

**Richard Louv**

# ❧ Life ❧

Life is either a daring adventure or nothing.

**Helen Keller**

Life is too short to be little.

**Benjamin Disraeli**

Life must be lived forwards, but can be only understood backwards.

**Soren Kierkegaad**

There is only one success: To be able to spend your life in your own way.

**Christopher Morley**

There is no cure for birth and death, save to enjoy the interval.

**George Santayana**

Begin at once to live and count each separate day as a separate life.

**Seneca**

Twenty years from now you will be more disappointed by the things you didn't do, than by the ones that you did do.

**H. Jackson Brown Jr.**

The goal of life is living in agreement with nature.

**Zend of Ditium**

Life is tough.
Three out of three people die, so shut up and deal.

**Ring Landner**

Life is really simple, but we insist on making it complicated.

**Confucius**

A life unexamined, is not worth living.

**Democritus**

Life is too important to be taken seriously.

**Oscar Wilde**

Sooner or later, a wise person discovers that life is:
a mixture of good days and bad; victory and defeat; give and take.

**Wilfred A. Peterson**

If you are not living on the edge, you are taking up too much room.

**James Whittaker**

There are three ingredients in the good life: learning, earning and yearning.

**Christopher Morley**

Accept both compliments and criticism.
It takes both sun and rain for a flower to grow.

**Marek Kośniowski**

Four rules for life:
Show up. Pay attention. Tell the truth. Don't be attached to the results.

**Angeles Arrien**

To be what we are, and to become what we are capable of becoming,
is the only end of life.

**Robert Louis Stevenson**

To fail to understand that life is going to knock you down,
is to fail to understand the Irishness of life.

**Daniel Patrick Moynihan**

I have found if you love life, life will love you back.

**Arthur Rubinstein**

Life's challenges are not supposed to paralyse you,
they're supposed to help you discover who you are.

**Bernice Johnson Reagon**

Be happy for this moment. This moment is your life.

**Omar Khayyam**

Life isn't about finding yourself, it's about creating yourself.

**George Bernard Shaw**

My mission in life is not merely to survive, but to thrive and to do so
with some passion, some compassion, some humour and some style.

**Maya Angelou**

Instead of wondering when your next vacation is,
maybe you should set up a life you don't need to escape from.

**Seth Godin**

Three things in life: your health, your mission and the people you love, that's it.

**Naval Ravikant**

Life is an echo, what you send out comes back.

**Chinese Proverb**

The shoe that fits one person pinches another; there is no recipe for living that suits all cases.

**Carl Jung**

Not a shred of evidence exists in favour of the idea that life is serious.

**Brendan Gill**

# Listening

Listen and silent contain the same letters.

**Alfred Brendel**

The first duty of love is to listen.

**Paul Tillich**

Hearing is one of the body's five senses, but listening is an art.

**Frank Tyger**

The art of conversation lies in listening.

**Malcolm Forbes**

When people talk, listen and listen completely.
Most people never listen.

**Ernest Hemingway**

The only way to entertain some folks is to listen to them.

**Frank Hubbard**

Lenin could listen so intently that he exhausted the speaker.

**Isaiah Berlin**

From listening comes wisdom and from speaking comes
repentance.

**Italian Proverb**

A good listener is not only popular everywhere,
but after a while they know something.

**Wilson Mizner**

Formula for handling people:
1. Listen to the other person's story.
2. Listen to the other person's full story.
3. Listen to the other person's full story first.

**George Marshall**

Take a tip from nature; your ears aren't made to be shut, but your mouth is.

**Anonymous**

One of the best ways to persuade others is by listening to them.

**Dean Rusk**

Silence, often misunderstood but never misquoted.

**Anonymous**

Sometimes you have to let silence do the heavy lifting.

**Susan Scott**

Too often, we underestimate the power of touch, a smile, a kind word, a listening ear,
an honest compliment or the smallest act of caring,
all of which have the potential to turn a life around.

**Leo Buscaglia**

When we listen, we hear someone into existence.

**Laurie Buchanan**

The opposite of talking isn't listening, the opposite of talking is waiting!

**Fran Lebowitz**

Listen with the will to learn.

**Unarine Ramaru**

Listen with your eyes as well as your ears.

**Graham Speechley**

Listen with your mouth closed and your heart open.

**Christine Toda**

Most of the successful people I've known are the ones who do more listening than talking.

**Bernard M. Baruch**

Wisdom is the reward you get for a lifetime of listening when you would have rather talked.

**Mark Twain**

Listening to and understanding our inner sufferings will resolve most of the problems we encounter.

**Thich Nhat Hanh**

The older I get, the more I listen to people who don't talk much.

**Germain G. Glidden**

Don't think or judge, just listen.

**Sarah Dessen**

# Love

A baby is born with a need to be loved and never outgrows it.

**Frank A. Clarke**

Love: two minds without a single thought.

**Philip Barry**

Love conquers all things: let us too surrender to love.

**Virgil**

Experience shows us that love does not consist in gazing at each other, but in looking together in the same direction.

**Antoine de Saint-Exupéry**

Pure love is a willingness to give without a thought of receiving anything in return.

**Peace Pilgrim**

In the arithmetic of love, one plus one equals everything and two minus one equals nothing.

**Mignon McLaughlin**

Love is what's left of a relationship after all the selfishness has been removed.

**Cullen Hightower**

To live without love is not really to live.

**Moliere**

A bell is not a bell until you ring it,
a song is not a song until you sing it.
Love in your heart is not put there to stay,
love is not love, until you give it away.

**Oscar Hammerstein II**

What the world really needs is more love and less paperwork.

**Pearl Bailey**

We can do no great things, only small things with great love.

**Mother Teresa**

I've learnt that love, not time, heals all wounds.

**Andrew Rooney**

Love and a cough cannot be hid.

**Latin Proverb**

Love is not the dying moan of a distant violin; it's the triumphant
twang of a bed spring.

**S. J. Perelman**

Those who love deeply never grow old; they may die of old age, but
they die young.

**Arthur Wing Pinero**

To love oneself is the beginning of a lifelong romance.

**Oscar Wilde**

Gestures in love, are incomparably more attractive, effective and
valuable than words.

**Francois Rabelais**

Love and compassion are necessities not luxuries;
without them humanity cannot survive.

**Dalai Lama**

Love does not dominate, it cultivates.

**Johann Wolfgang Von Goethe**

Love recognises no barriers.

**Maya Angelou**

You don't marry someone you can live with,
you marry someone you cannot live without.

**Anonymous**

Come live in my heart and pay no rent.

**Samuel Lover**

Loving someone means helping them to be more themselves,
which can be different from being what you'd like them to be,
although often they turn out the same.

**Merle Shain**

We forgive, so long as we love.

**Francois De La Rochefoucauld**

The way to love anything is to realise that it might be lost.

**G. K. Chesterton**

#  Money

Money is a terrible master but an excellent servant.

**P. T. Barnum**

Make money your God and it will plague you like the devil.

**Henry Fielding**

They, will always be a slave, who do not know how to live upon a little.

**Horace**

A wise person should have money in the head, but not in their heart.

**Jonathan Swift**

What's money?
A man is a success if he gets up in the morning and goes to bed in the evening and in between does what he wants to do.

**Bob Dylan**

There is no amount of money in the world that will make you comfortable if you are not comfortable with yourself.

**Stuart Wilde**

Frugality is a great income.

**Cicero**

I don't like money actually, but it quiets my nerves.

**Joe Louis**

One should look down on money, but never lose sight of it.

**Andre Prevot**

They, who are of the opinion that money will do everything,
may very well be suspected to do everything for money.

**George Saville**

Money speaks sense in a language of all nations.

**Aphra Beun**

It is possible to own too much.
A man with one watch knows what time it is.
A man with two watches is never quite sure.

**Lee Segall**

It is said that for money you can have everything, but you cannot.
You can buy food, but not appetite; medicine, but not health;
knowledge, but not wisdom; glitter, but not beauty;
fun, but not joy; acquaintances, but not friends;
servants, but not faithfulness; leisure, but not peace.
You can have the husk of everything for money, but not the kernel.

**Arne Garborg**

Pola Debevoise:        I want to marry Rockefeller.
Schatze Page:          Which one?
Pola Debevoise:        I don't care.

Owning a home is a keystone of wealth, giving both financial and
emotional security.

**Suze Orman**

Beware of little expenses; a small leak will sink a great ship.

**Benjamin Graham**

Formerly, when great fortunes were only made in war, war was a business; but now,
when great fortunes are only made by business, business is war.

**Christian Mestell Bovee**

A business that makes nothing but money is a poor business.

**Henry Ford**

Philanthropy is commendable but it must not cause the Philanthropist to overlook the circumstances which makes philanthropy necessary.

**Martin Luther King**

Debt is the prolific mother of folly and crime.

**Benjamin Disraeli**

Financial peace isn't the acquisition of stuff.
It's learning to live on less than you make, so you can give money back and have money to invest.
You can't win until you do this.

**David Ramsey**

Solvency is entirely a matter of temperament and not income.

**Logan Pearsall Smith**

Cocaine is God's way of telling you, you've too much money.

**Gordon Sumner**

But ah! Think of what you do when you run in debt:
you give to another, power over your liberty.

**Benjamin Franklin**

The five second M.B.A.: Have more money coming in, than going out.

**Tadhg McCarthy**

I believe that banking institutions are more dangerous to our liberties
than standing armies.

**Thomas Jefferson**

I cannot afford to waste my time making money.

**Louis Agassiz**

Resolve not to be poor.
Whatever you have, spend less.
Poverty is a great enemy to human happiness.
It certainly destroys liberty.

**Samuel Johnson**

How did the fool and the money get together in the first place?

**Steven Wright**

#  Music

Without music, life would be a mistake.

**Friedrich Nietzsche**

If music be the food of love, play on.

**William Shakespeare**

Music expresses that which cannot be said and on which, it is impossible to be silent.

**Victor Hugo**

What we play is life.

**Louis Armstrong**

Music is the language spoken by angels.

**Henry Longfellow**

Music is the only sensual pleasure without vice.

**Samuel Johnson**

I often think in music, I live my daydreams in music,
I see my life in terms of music; I get most joy in life out of my violin.

**Albert Einstein**

Anything that is too stupid to be spoken is sung.

**Voltaire**

Handel is so great and so simple that no one but a professional musician is unable to understand him.

**Samuel Butler**

Mozart roused my admiration when I was young;
he caused me to despair when I reached maturity;
he is now the comfort of my old age.

**Gioachino Rossini**

Fame and rest are utter opposites.

**Richard Steele**

I only know two tunes, one is Yankee Doodle and the other isn't.

**Ulysses S. Grant**

The notes I handle no better than many pianists.
But the pauses between the notes – Ah, that is where the art resides.

**Arthur Schnabel**

There is no feeling, except the extremes of fear and grief,
that does not find relief in music.

**George Eliot**

Music is the arithmetic of sounds, as optics is the geometry of light.

**Claude Debussy**

Music is the divine way to tell beautiful poetic things to the heart.

**Pablo Casals**

Country music is three cords and the truth.

**Marlan Howard**

Bach is the immortal God of harmony.

**Ludwig Van Beethoven**

Wagner has lovely moments, but awful quarters of an hour.

**Gioacchino Rossini**

Music is the best means we have of digesting time.

**W. H. Auden**

Music, once admitted to the soul, becomes a sort of spirit and never dies.

**Edward Bulwer-Lytton**

Music can name the unnameable and communicate the unknowable.

**Leonard Bernstein**

I haven't understood a bar of music in my life, but I have felt it.

**Igor Stravinsky**

Music drives you. It wakes you up, it gets you pumping
and at the end of the day, the correct tune will chill you down.

**Dimebag Darrell**

Music is an outburst of the soul.

**Frederick Delius**

# ✺ Nature ✺

The goal of life is living in agreement with nature.

**Zeno**

The earth laughs in flowers.

**Ralph Waldo Emerson**

Everything has beauty, but not everyone sees it.

**Confucius**

The summer night is like a perfection of thought.

**Wallace Stevens**

He who plants trees, loves others besides himself.

**Thomas Fuller**

We may brave human laws, but we cannot resist natural ones.

**Jules Verne**

The fairest thing in nature, a flower, still has its roots in earth and manure.

**D. H. Lawrence**

After reading Thoreau, I felt how much I have lost by leaving nature out of my life.

**F. Scott Fitzgerald**

The guy who wrote "a job well done never needs doing again" never weeded a garden.

**Anonymous**

The 3 great elemental sounds in nature are:
the sound of rain, the sound of wind in the primeval wood and
the sound of outer ocean on a beach.

**Henry Beston**

Nature uses as little as possible of anything.

**Johannes Kepler**

Never does nature say one thing and wisdom another.

**Juvenal**

Those who contemplate the beauty of the earth
find reserves of strength that will endure as long as life lasts.

**Rachel Carson**

Look deep into nature and then you will understand everything
better.

**Albert Einstein**

The day, water, sun, moon, night –
I do not have to purchase these things with money.

**Plautus**

If the English language made any sense, lackadaisical would
have something to do with a shortage of flowers.

**Doug Larson**

Let us permit nature to have her way. She understands her business
better than we do.

**Michel De Montaigne**

To the artist, there is never anything ugly in nature.

**August Rodin**

Nature to be commanded must be obeyed.

**Francis Bacon**

Nature does not hurry, yet everything is accomplished.

**Lao Tzu**

Whoever loves and understands a garden will find contentment within.

**Chinese Proverb**

Take a quiet walk with Mother Nature.
It will nurture your mind, body and soul.

**A. D. Williams**

Choose only one master – nature.

**Rembrandt**

Adopt the pace of nature: her secret is patience.

**Ralph Waldo Emerson**

# Old Age

Growing old is mandatory; growing up is optional.

**Chili Davis**

The great thing about getting older, is that you don't lose all the other ages you've been.

**Madeleine L'Engle**

Once you are over the hill, you begin to pick up speed.

**Charles M. Schulz**

If I had my life to live over again, I'd make the same mistakes, only sooner.

**Tullulah Bankhead**

Everyone is the age of their heart.

**Guatemalan Proverb**

We don't stop playing because we grow old,
we grow old because we stop playing.

**George Bernard Shaw**

At 20, we worry about what others think of us;
at 40, we don't care about what others think of us;
at 60, we discover they haven't been thinking about us at all.

**Anonymous**

Age is the acceptance of a term of years, but maturity is the glory of years.

**Martha Graham**

There is still no cure for the common birthday.

**John Glenn**

The three stages of life:
youth, middle age and you're looking great.

**Nelson Rockefeller**

Growing old is no more than a bad habit, which a busy person has no time for.

**André Maurois**

A beautiful body and a beautiful face age, grow old.
A beautiful mind does not age and in fact can become ever more beautiful.

**Edward de Bono**

No one grows old by living, only by losing interest in living.

**Marie Beynon Ray**

Given three requisites –
means of existence, reasonable health and an absorbing interest –
those years beyond 60 can be the happiest and most satisfying of a lifetime.

**Earnest Elmo Calkins**

If you want to know how old a woman is, ask her sister-in-law.

**E. W. Howe**

Old age is an excellent time for outrage.
My goal is to say or do at least one outrageous thing every week.

**Maggie Kuhn**

I am content in my later years. I have kept my good humour and take neither myself nor the next person seriously.

**Albert Einstein**

Age is something that doesn't matter, unless you are a cheese.

**Billie Burke**

I think myself, that age is to a certain degree a habit.

**Benjamin Disraeli**

Whatever a man's age, he can reduce it several years by putting a bright-coloured flower in his button-hole.

**Mark Twain**

The longer I live the more beautiful life becomes.

**Frank Lloyd Wright**

Grow old along with me. The best is yet to come.

**Robert Browning**

What is that unforgettable line?

**Samuel Beckett**

I love everything that is old: old friends, old times, old manners, old books, old wine.

**Oliver Goldsmith**

The best cosmetic in the world is an active mind that is always finding something new.

**Mary Meek Atkeson**

Death is the penalty we all have to pay for the privilege of life.

**Robert Half**

The fear of death keeps us from living, not from dying.

**Paul C. Roud**

To be able to enjoy one's past is to live twice.

**Martial Gueroult**

# ✵ Optimism ✵

Choose to be optimistic; it feels better.

**Dalai Lama**

Optimism - the doctrine or belief that everything is beautiful,
including what is ugly.

**Ambrose Bierce**

Optimism is the faith that leads to achievement;
nothing can be done without hope and confidence.

**Helen Keller**

Perpetual optimism is a force multiplier.

**Colin Powell**

Pessimism leads to weakness, optimism to power.

**William James**

Optimism is the foundation of courage.

**Nicholas M. Butler**

Optimism means better than reality. Pessimism means worse than reality.
I am a realist.

**Margaret Atwood**

The optimist proclaims that we live in the best of all possible worlds;
the pessimist fears this is true.

**James Branch Cabell**

For myself I am an optimist, it does not seem to be much use to be anything else.

**Winston Churchill**

If you can't give children optimism, then what are you doing?

**Matt Haig**

For me, optimism is two lovers walking into the sunset arm in arm. Or maybe into the sunrise, whatever appeals to you.

**Krzysztof Kieslowski**

You must not lose faith in humanity. Humanity is an ocean. If a few drops are dirty, the ocean does not become dirty.

**Mahatma Gandhi**

My dear friends, clear your mind of can't.

**Samuel Johnson**

Sometimes when you are in a dark place, you think you've been buried, but you've actually been planted.

**Christine Caine**

Never regret a day in your life:
good days give happiness, bad days give experience,
worst days give lessons and the best days give memories.

**Elizabeth Farrell**

Optimism makes a life happier and meaningful.

**M. K. Soni**

It's not that optimism solves all of life's problems:
it is just that it can sometimes make the difference between coping
and collapsing.

**Lucy MacDonald**


Optimism inspires, energises and brings out our best.
It points the mind towards possibilities and helps us think creatively
past problems.

**Price Pritchett**


Some people grumble that roses have thorns;
I am grateful that thorns have roses.

**Alphonse Karr**


Pessimism never won any battles.

**Dwight D. Eisenhower**


I am a pessimist because of intelligence,
 but an optimist because of will.

**Antonio Gramsci**


Both optimists and pessimists contribute to society.
The optimist invented the aeroplane, the pessimist the parachute.

**George Bernard Shaw**


Everything's gonna be alright.

**Bob Marley**

# ❧ Patience ❧

Patience is the companion of Wisdom.

**St. Augustine**

Have patience; all things are difficult before they become easy.

**Sadi**

Genius is eternal patience.

**Michelangelo**

Patience is bitter, but its fruits are sweet.

**Jean-Jacques Rousseau**

Patience strengthens the spirit, sweetens the temper, stifles anger, extinguishes envy, subdues pride, bridles the tongue.

**George Horne**

If you are patient in a moment of anger, you will escape a hundred days of sorrow.

**Chinese Proverb**

Patience, that blending of moral courage with physical timidity.

**Thomas Hardy**

Impatient people always arrive too late.

**Jean Dutourd**

In prosperity, caution; In adversity, patience.

**Dutch Proverb**

In any contest between power and patience, bet on patience.

**W. B. Prescott**

Impatience never commanded success.

**Edwin H. Chapin**

Patience and time do more than strength and passion.

**Jean De La Fontaine**

It is not necessary for all people to be great in action.
The greatest and sublimest power is often simple patience.

**Horace Bushnell**

Whether it's marriage or business, patience is the first rule of
success.

**William Feather**

A wise person does not try to hurry history.
Many wars have been avoided by patience and
many have been precipitated by reckless haste.

**Adlai Stevenson**

Patience is a conquering virtue.

**Geoffrey Chaucer**

The secret of patience is to do something else in the meantime.

**Croft M. Pentz**

Patience, persistence and perspiration make an unbeatable
combination for success.

**Napoleon Hill**

The trees that are slow to grow bear the best fruit.

**Moliere**

Patience is necessary and one cannot reap immediately where one has sown.

**Soren Kierkegaard**

Have patience with all things, but first of all with yourself.

**St. Francis de Sales**

# Present

Only in the present do things happen.

**Jorge Luis Borges**

The future is now.

**Burton Benjamin**

'Now' is the watchword of the wise.

**Charles H. Spurgeon**

You must live in the present, launch yourself on every wave,
find your eternity in each moment.

**Henry David Thoreau**

Our grand business is not to see what lies dimly in the distance,
but to do what lies clearly at hand.

**Thomas Carlyle**

Everyone's life lies within the present;
for the past is spent and done with and the future is uncertain.

**Marcus Antonius**

Today well lived, makes every yesterday a happy memory and
every tomorrow a vision of hope.

**Kalidasa**

The great rule of moral conduct is, next to God, to respect time.

**Johann Lavater**

If you are depressed, you are living in the past;
if you are anxious, you are living in the future;
if you are at peace, you are living in the present.

**Lao Tzu**

I never think of the future; it comes soon enough.

**Albert Einstein**

I have no yesterdays, time took them away,
tomorrow may not be, but I have today.

**Pearl Yeadon McGinnis**

How we spend our days, is how we spend our lives.

**Annie Dillard**

Present time is a circus, always packing up and moving away.

**Ben Hetch**

I went to a restaurant that serves "breakfast at any time",
so I ordered French toast during the Renaissance.

**Steven Wright**

Eat the present moment and break the dish.

**Egyptian Proverb**

The innocent and the beautiful have no enemy but time.

**William Butler Yeats**

Today is the pupil of yesterday.

**Publilius Syrus**

Take time to think – it is the source of power
Take time to play – it is the secret of perpetual youth
Take time to read – it is the fountain of wisdom
Take time to pray – it is the greatest power on earth
Take time to love – it is the God given privilege
Take time to be friendly – it is the road to happiness
Take time to laugh – it is the music of the soul
Take time to give – it is too short a day to be selfish
Take time to work – it is the price of success

**Martin Greyford**


The ability to be in the present, is a major component of mental wellness.

**Abraham Maslow**


Life gives you plenty of time to do whatever you want to do,
if you stay in the present moment.

**Deepak Chopra**


Yesterday is history, tomorrow is a mystery.
Today is a gift, that is why it is called the present.

**Alice Morse Earle**


Your life requires your mindful presence in order to live it. Be here now.

**Akiroq Brost**


Wherever you are, be all there.

**James Elliot**


The future is purchased by the present.

**Samuel Johnson**

Forget past mistakes, forget failures.

Forget everything except what you're going to do right now.

**William Durant**

Hold every moment sacred.

**Thomas Mann**

# Problems

Problems are fuel for improvement.

**Ray Dalio**

The problem is the problem, the person is not the problem.

**Michael White & David Epston**

There are not problems in life, just challenges.

**Dinis Guarda**

You can overcome anything, if you don't bellyache.

**Bernard M. Baruch**

Every age has its problems, by solving which, humanity is helped forward.

**Heinrich Heine**

The most important thing to do in solving a problem is to begin.

**Frank Tyger**

The second assault on the same problem should come from a totally different direction.

**Tom Hirshfield**

The problem is not that there are problems.
The problem is expecting otherwise and thinking that having problems is a problem.

**Theodore Rubin**

Some people approach every problem with an open mouth.

**Adlai Stevenson**

Life is not a problem to be solved, but a mystery to be lived.

**Thomas Merton**

Out of suffering have emerged the strongest souls.

**E. H. Chapin**

One of the disadvantages of wine is that it makes one mistake words for thoughts.

**Samuel Johnson**

Burdens become light when cheerfully borne.

**Ovid**

You've got to take the bull by the teeth!

**Samuel Goldwyn**

Problems cannot be solved at the same level of thinking that created them.

**Albert Einstein**

You must learn from the mistakes of others.
You can't possibly live long enough to make them all yourself.

**Samuel Levenson**

Fixing problems is actually a lot easier than not fixing them, because not fixing them will make you miserable.

**Ray Dalio**

You can't change the cards life has dealt you,
but you can determine the way you'll play them.

**Ty Boyd**

A problem is a chance for you to do your best.

**Duke Ellington**

Problems are not stop signs, they are guidelines.

**Robert Schuller**

There is no magic wand that can solve our problems.
The solution rests with our work and discipline.

**Jose Eduardo dos Santos**

Others can stop you temporarily; you are the only one to do it
permanently.

**Zig Ziglar**

Most of the problems in life are for 2 reasons:
we act without thinking or we keep thinking without acting.

**Zig Ziglar**

When I go to bed, I leave my troubles with my clothes.

**Dutch Proverb**

Behind every argument is someone's ignorance.

**Louis D. Brandeis**

Don't agonise, organise.

**Florynce Kennedy**

No problem is too big to run away from.

**Charles M. Schulz**

In difficult and hopeless situations, the boldest plans are the safest.

**Titus Livy**

I am more important than my problems.

**José Ferrer**

The way most people fail, is in not keeping up heart.

**Lady Augusta Gregory**

The world is full of suffering. It is also full of the overcoming of it.

**Helen Keller**

If there was nothing wrong in the world, there wouldn't be anything for us to do.

**George Bernard Shaw**

# Purpose

Purpose is what gives life a meaning.

**C. H. Parkhurst**

The meaning of life is to find your gift; the purpose of life is to give it away.

**Pablo Picasso**

The purpose of life is doing your best at what you are best at, for the benefit of others.

**Charles Handy**

Find a purpose in life so big, it will challenge every capacity to be at your best.

**David O. McKay**

Live your life as though your every act were to become a universal law.

**Immanuel Kant**

Give one health and a course to steer;
and they will never stop to trouble about whether they're happy or not.

**George Bernard Shaw**

The purpose of life is not to be happy; it is to be useful,
to be honourable, to be compassionate,
to have it make some difference that you have lived and lived well.

**Ralph Waldo Emerson**

We are here on earth to do good to others.
What others are here for, I don't know.

**W. H. Auden**

Every action of our lives touches on some chord that will vibrate in eternity.

**Sean O'Casey**

The 2 most important days in your life:
the day you were born and the day you discover the reason why.

**Mark Twain**

Remember that wherever your heart is, there you will find your treasure.

**Paulo Coelmo**

We are products of our past, but we don't have to be prisoners of it.

**Rick Warren**

Everyone has a purpose in life, a unique gift or special talent to give to others.
And when we blend this unique talent with services to others,
we experience the ecstasy and exultation of our own spirit,
which is the ultimate goal of goals.

**Deepak Chopra**

Sooner or later, we must realise there is no station, no one place to arrive at once and for all. The true joy of life is the trip.

**Robert J. Hastings**

The secret of success is consistency of purpose.

**Benjamin Disraeli**

When a person can't find a deep sense of meaning, they distract themselves with pleasure.

**Viktor Frankl**

Everything is held together with stories.
That is all that is holding us together, stories and compassion.

**Barry Lopez**


Follow your dreams; they know the way.

**Kobe Yamada**


When you walk in purpose, you collide with destiny.

**Ralph Buchanan**


Let the beauty of what you love be what you do.

**Rumi**


A clear purpose will unite you as you move forward,
values will guide your behaviour and
goals will focus your energy.

**Kenneth H. Blanchard**

# Reputation

A person has 3 names:
The name they inherit, the name their parents give them and
the name they make for themselves.

**Les Brown**

Regard your good name as the richest jewel you can possibly be
possessed of.
The way to gain a good reputation is to endeavour to be what you
desire to appear.

**Socrates**

Reputations are longer in the making than the losing.

**Paul Von Ringelheim**

You can't build a reputation on what you are going to do.

**Henry Ford**

Associate yourself with people of good quality,
for 'tis better to be alone than in bad company.

**Booker T. Washington**

What people say behind your back is your standing in the community.

**E. W. Howe**

A reputation is rarely enhanced by an autobiography.

**T. K. Whitaker**

The great difficulty is first to win a reputation;
the next to keep it while you live;
and the next, to preserve it after you die.

**Benjamin Maydon**

Glass, china and reputation are easily cracked and never well mended.

**Benjamin Grahan**

### Family Name

You got it from your Father, it was all he had to give.
So it's yours to use and cherish, for as long as you may live.

If you lose the watch he gave you, it can always be replaced.
But a black mark on your name, son, can never be erased.

It was clean the day you took it, and a worthy name to bear.
When he got it from his Father, there was no dishonour there.

So make sure you guard it wisely, after all is said and done.
You'll be glad the name is spotless, when you give it to your son.

**Edgar A. Guest**

You can't buy a good reputation; you must earn it.

**Harvey Mackey**

Live in such a way that you would not be ashamed to sell your parrot
to the town gossip.

**Will Rogers**

Always do what is right; it will gratify half of mankind and astound
the other.

**Mark Twain**

A reputation as a hard worker is a good reputation.

**Kevin Hart**

I rather like my reputation, actually, that of a spoiled genius from the Welsh gutter,
a drunk, a womanizer; its rather an attractive image.

**Richard Burton**

A single lie destroys a whole reputation for integrity.

**Baltasar**

Self-esteem is the reputation you have with yourself.

**Brian Tracy**

Remember that reputation and integrity are your most valuable assets and can be lost in a heartbeat.

**Charles T. Munger**

Spend your time designing the greatest reputation one could have.

**Christopher Murray**

It is the duty of everyone to strive to gain and deserve a good reputation.

**Francis Atterbury**

Be yourself. The world worships the original.

**Ingrid Bergman**

The best inheritance parents can leave a child is a good name.

**Verne McLellan**

#  Respect

Respect yourself and others will respect you.

**Confucius**

There is no respect for others, without humility in oneself.

**Frédéric Amiel**

I cannot conceive of a greater loss, than the loss of one's self-respect.

**Mahatma Gandhi**

When you practice gratefulness, there is a sense of respect towards others.

**Dalai Lama**

Respect for ourselves guides our morals;
respect for others guides our manners.

**Laurence Sterne**

Most good relationships are built on mutual trust and respect.

**Mona Sutphen**

The surest test of an individual's integrity is their refusal to do
or say anything that would damage their self-respect.

**Thomas S. Monson**

A person is a person, no matter how small.

**Theodor Geisel**

The respect of those you respect, is worth more than the applause of the multitude.

**Arnold Glasow**

Having the courage to live within one's means is respectability.

**Benjamin Disraeli**

Customer: have you anything for grey hair?
Conscientious Druggist: nothing, Madam, but the greatest respect.

**Herbert V. Prochnow**

To the living we owe respect, but to the dead we owe only the truth.

**Voltaire**

Everyone has an invisible sign hanging from their neck saying: "make me feel important".

**Mary Kay Ash**

If we are not free, no one will respect us.

**A. P. J. Abdul Kalam**

When you are content to be simply yourself and don't compare or compete, everybody will respect you.

**Lao Tzu**

Show respect to all people, but grovel to none.

**Tecumseh**

Respect comes in two unchangeable steps: giving it and receiving it.

**Edmond Mbiaka**

Respect begins with this attitude:
I acknowledge that you are a creature of extreme worth.

**Gary Chapman**

Life is short and we should respect every moment of it.

**Orhan Pamuk**

Attitude is a choice. Happiness is a choice. Kindness is a choice.
Giving is a choice. Respect is a choice.
Whatever choice you make, makes you. Choose wisely.

**Roy T. Bennett**

"I was wrong", builds more respect than "I told you so".

**Daniel Rockwell**

It is mutual respect which makes friendship lasting.

**John Henry Newman**

What women want is what men want. They want respect.

**Marilyn Vos Savant**

# Responsibility

I believe I have a personal responsibility to make a positive impact on society.
**Anthony Fauci**

The greatest day in our life is when we take total responsibility for our attitudes. That's the day we truly grow up.
**John C. Maxwell**

Leadership is about vision and responsibility, not power.
**Seth Berkley**

Hold yourself responsible for a higher standard than anybody else expects of you.
Never excuse yourself.
**Henry Ward Beecher**

You can't escape the responsibility of tomorrow by evading it today.
**Abraham Lincoln**

We are not put here on earth to play around; there is work to be done. There are responsibilities to be met. Humanity needs the ability of every man and woman.
**Aiden Palmer**

It is easy to dodge our responsibilities, but we cannot dodge the consequences of dodging our responsibilities.
**Josiah Stamp**

People who do things without being told draw the most wages.
**Edwin H. Stuart**

If you want to keep your children's feet on the ground, put some responsibility on their shoulders.

**Abigail Van Buren**

Privilege and responsibility are two sides of the same coin.

**Vern McLellan**

When your shoulders are carrying a load of responsibility, there isn't room for chips.

**Anonymous**

The ability to accept responsibility is the measure of an individual.

**Roy L. Smith**

The greatest gifts you can give your children are the roots of responsibility and the wings of independence.

**Denis Waitley**

A nation is formed by the willingness of each of us to share in the responsibility for upholding the common good.

**Barbara Jordan**

You become responsible forever, for what you have tamed.

**Antoine de Saint-Exupéry**

A step backward, after making a wrong turn, is a step in the right direction.

**Kurt Vonnegut**

Freedom is the will to be responsible for ourselves.

**Friedrich Nietzsche**

The victim mindset dilutes the human potential.
By not accepting personal responsibility for our circumstances,
we greatly reduce our power to change them.

**Stephen Maraboli**

Action springs not from thought, but from a readiness for
responsibility.

**Dietrich Bonhoeffer**

If you can take responsibility for your own life,
then you will begin to realise that you can change it.

**H. K. Abell**

Happiness is your responsibility.
If you depend or wait for other people to make you happy, you will
always be disappointed.

**Byron Pulsifer**

To achieve life mastery and be worthy of a life well lived,
we must take action, ownership and responsibility for our choices.

**William Craig**

No one gets away with anything, ever, so take responsibility for your
own life.

**Jordan Peterson**

# Security

Security is knowing that someone cares whether you are or cease to be.

**Malcolm Forbes**

Only in growth, reform and change, paradoxically enough, is true security to be found.

**Anne Morrow Lindbergh**

Growth demands a temporary surrender of security.

**Gail Sheehy**

There is no security on this earth; there is only opportunity.

**Douglas MacArthur**

The ultimate security is your understanding of reality.

**H. Stanley Judd**

When you know that you're capable of dealing with whatever comes, you have the only security the world has to offer.

**Harold Browne**

It is only when we all play safe that we create a world of utmost insecurity.

**Dag Hammarskjold**

The trouble with worrying so much about your security in the future, is that you feel so insecure in the present.

**Harlan Miller**

The desire for safety stands against every great and noble enterprise.

**Tacitus**


Security is when everything is settled. When nothing can happen to you.
Security is denial of life.

**Germaine Greer**


The fact is people are good.
Give people affection and security, and they will give affection
and be secure in their feelings and their behaviour.

**Abraham Maslow**


Nothing can bring a real sense of security into the home except true love.

**Billy Graham**


If you want total security, go to prison.
There you're fed, clothed, given medical care and so on.
The only thing lacking........ is freedom.

**Dwight D. Eisenhower**


Do not confuse security with certainty.
The man who knows he will be hanged tomorrow has certainty, but
not security.

**John Kay**


The person who can easily define their weaknesses, their faults,
is able to self-deprecate, that person is secure, feels secure
and happy within their own skin.

**Robert Black**


The real security in life are the skills you have and
the people you know.

**Anonymous**

Money is a necessity, but not the determinant of a successful life.
It is there to secure you, but not to save you.
It is there to support you, but not to sanctify you.

**Israelmore Ayivor**

Do exactly what you would do if you felt more secure.

**Meister Eckhart**

We should never forget the inevitable, as we will lose everything eventually.
So, why fret over any kind of security?
The idea is to just fly and experience it all while it lasts.

**Sushant Singh Rajput**

All people want is to be safe and feel loved.

**Bryant McGill**

Security represents your sense of worth, your identity, your
emotional anchorage, your basic personal strength or lack of it.

**Stephen Covey**

The more you seek security, the less of it you have.
But the more you seek opportunity, the more likely
it is that you will achieve the security you desire.

**Brian Tracy**

The task we must set ourselves is not to feel secure but to be able to
tolerate insecurity.

**Erich Fromm**

We must have courage to bet on our ideas,
to take the calculated risk and to act.

**Maxwell Maltz**

True security lies in trying new things, reading new books, meeting new people, thinking new thoughts and taking greater risks.

**Robin Sharma**

A bird in a nest is secure, but this is not why God gave it wings.

**Matshona Dhliwayo**

# ❦ Speaking ❦

Don't speak unless you can improve the silence.

**Jorge Luis Borges**

In order to speak short upon any subject, think long.

**H. H. Brackenridge**

First learn the meaning of what you say and then speak.

**Epictetus**

To say nothing often reflects a fine command of the English language.

**Robert Benchley**

When you are angry, say nothing and do nothing until you have recited the alphabet.

**Athenodorous Cananites**

The less you talk, the more you are listened to.

**Abigail Von Buren**

Nothing is often a good thing to do and always a clever thing to say.

**William Durant**

There are very few people who don't become more interesting when they stop talking.

**Mary Lowry**

Wisdom is divided into 2 parts:
1. Having a great deal to say; and 2. Not saying it.

**Thomas Fuller**

The trouble with speaking too fast is you may say something you haven't thought of yet.

**Ann Landers**

Never make a promise in haste.

**Mahatma Gandhi**

I disapprove of what you say, but I will defend to the death your right to say it.

**Voltaire**

Eloquence: saying the proper thing and stopping.

**Francois de la Rochefoucauld**

Talk is cheap because supply exceeds demand.
A word, once let out of the cage, cannot be whistled back again.

**Horace**

If I kept my mouth shut, I wouldn't be here.

**Sign under a Mounted Fish**

The object of oratory is not truth but persuasion.

**Thomas Babington MacAuley**

The world is shaped by two things, stories told and the memories left behind.

**Vera Nazarian**

Diplomacy is the language of international relations,
which can say one thing and has two absolutely opposite meanings.

**Dalton Trumbo**

The human brain starts working the moment you are born
and never stops until you stand up to speak in public.

**George Jessel**

If your mind goes blank, be sure to turn off the sound.

**Steven Smith**

Words are clothes thoughts wear.

**Samuel Beckett**

Many a man's tongue broke his nose.

**Seamus MacManus**

Don't talk about yourself; it will be done when you leave.

**Addison Mizner**

Slander cannot destroy one. When the flood recedes, the rock is still
there.

**Chinese Proverb**

Where you see wrong or inequality or injustice, speak out, because
this is your country.
This is your democracy. Make it, protect it, pass it on.

**Thurgood Marshall**

Listen with curiosity. Speak with honesty. Act with integrity.

**Roy Bennett**

Before you speak T.H.I.N.K.:-
Is it true,
is it helpful,
is it inspiring,
is it necessary,
is it kind?

**Fran Lebowitz**


A discussion should be a genuine attempt to explore a subject
rather than a battle between competing egos.

**Edward de Bono**


Teach thy tongue to say: "I do not know".

**Maimonides**


Words are loaded pistols.

**Jean-Paul Sartre**

# ～ Tax ～

The hardest thing in the world to understand is the income tax.

**Albert Einstein**

When making your own income tax, it's better to give than deceive.

**Arnold Glasow**

Taxes grow without rain.

**Jewish Proverb**

The art of taxation consists in so plucking the goose as to obtain
the largest amount of feathers with the least amount of hissing.

**Jean Baptiste Colbert**

The Tax Payer: someone who works for the Government
but doesn't have to take a Civil Service Examination.

**Ronald Reagan**

A Citizen can hardly distinguish between a tax and a fine,
except that a fine is generally much lighter.

**G. K. Chesterton**

The art of Government is to make two-thirds of the nation
pay all it possibly can for the benefit of the other third.

**Voltaire**

Taxation is the price which civilised communities pay for the
opportunity of remaining civilised.

**Albert Bushnell Hart**

Inflation is taxation without representation.

**James T. Kesterson**

We must care for each other more and tax each other less.

**William Archer**

Collecting more taxes than is absolutely necessary, is legalised robbery.

**Calvin Coolidge**

In the first year the income tax paper arrived and I filled it up to show I was not liable.
They returned the paper with "most unsatisfactory" scrawled across it.
I wrote "I entirely agree" under the words and returning it once more.

**Arthur Conan Doyle**

Death and taxes may be inevitable, but they shouldn't be related.

**J. C. Watts**

The payment of taxes gives a right to protection.

**James M. Wayne**

What the Government gives, it must first take away.

**John S. Coleman**

The people are hungry: those in authority eat up too much taxes.

**Lao Tzu**

Philosophy teaches a man that he can't take it with him;
taxes teach him he can't leave it behind either.

**Mignon McLaughlin**


I think of lotteries as a tax on the mathematically challenged.

**Roger Jones**


The Government's view of the economy could be summed up in a
few short phrases:
If it moves, tax it. If it keeps moving, regulate it.
And if it stops moving, subsidise it.

**Ronald Reagan**


The difference between tax avoidance (legal) and tax evasion (illegal)
is the thickness of the prison wall.

**Denis Healey**


Death is the most convenient time to tax rich people.

**David Lloyd George**


Next to being shot at and missed, nothing is quite as satisfying as an
income tax refund.

**Terence Pratchett**


You get out of life what you put into it, minus the taxes.

**Al Lerreri**

# Technology

Humans are still the most extraordinary computers of all.

**John F. Kennedy**

Technology is best when it brings people together.

**Matthew Mullenweg**

Technology like art is a soaring exercise of the human imagination.

**Daniel Bell**

The technology you use impresses no one. The experience you create with it is everything.

**Sean Gerety**

Technology is a useful servant, but a dangerous master.

**Christian Lous Lange**

Technology should improve your life, not become your life.

**William Cox**

Technology: it is said one machine can do the work of
50 ordinary men.
No machine, however can do the work of one extraordinary man.

**Hsieh Tehyi**

People are only as good as their technical development allows them to be.

**George Orwell**

Technology is so much fun, but we can drown in our technology.
The fog of information can drive out knowledge.

**Daniel Boorstin**

Progress in science depends on new techniques, new discoveries
and new ideas, probably in that order.

**Sydney Brenner**

The factory of the future will have only 2 employees, a human and a dog.
The human will be there to feed the dog.
The dog will be there to stop the human touching the equipment.

**Warren Bennis**

Once a new technology rolls over you, if you're not part of the
steamroller, you're part of the road.

**Stewart Brand**

The real problem is not whether machines think, but whether men do.

**B. F. Skinner**

If we continue to develop our technology without wisdom or prudence,
our servant may prove to be our executioner.

**Omar N. Bradley**

Technology like art is a soaring exercise of the human imagination.

**Daniel Bell**

All the biggest technological inventions created by man –
The Airplane, The Automobile, The Computer – says little about his
intelligence, but speaks volumes about his laziness.

**Mark Kennedy**

The great growling engine of change – Technology.

**Alvin Toffler**

I force people to have a coffee with me, because I don't trust that a friendship can be maintained without any other senses besides a computer or cellphone screen.

**John Cusack**

If you don't innovate fast, disrupt your industry, disrupt yourself, you'll be left behind.

**John Chambers**

Computers are useless; they can only give you answers.

**Pablo Picasso**

Science and technology revolutionise our lives,
but memory, tradition and myth frame our response.

**Anonymous**

All the technology in the world will never replace a positive attitude.

**Harvey Mackay**

Simplicity is about subtracting the obvious and adding the meaningful.

**John Maeda**

Books don't need batteries.

**Nadine Gordimer**

People who smile while they are alone used to be called insane, until we invented smart phones and social media.

**Mokokoma Mokhonoana**

# Thinking/Thoughts

Don't believe everything you think.

**Robert Falghum**

The happiness of your life depends upon the quality of your thoughts.

**Marcus Aurelius Antoninus**

What we think, we become.

**Budda**

Thinking is the talking of the soul with itself.

**Plato**

People do not like to think. If one thinks, one must reach conclusions. Conclusions are not always pleasant.

**Helen Keller**

It is the mark of an educated person, to be able to entertain a thought without accepting it.

**Aristotle**

Think wrongly, if you please, but in all cases think for yourself.

**Doris Lessing**

Minds are like parachutes, they only function when they are open.

**James Dewar**

Always remember to bound thy thoughts to the present occasion.

**William Penn**

What I have done is due to patient thought.

Issac Newton

Second thoughts are even wiser.

Euripides

Our thoughts are often worse than we are.

George Eliot

One is not idle because they are absorbed in thought.
There is visible labour and there is invisible labour.

Victor Hugo

Bad terminology is the enemy of good thinking.

Warren Buffett

The brain can be developed just the same way as muscles can be
developed, if one will only take the pains to train the mind to think.

Thomas Alva Edison

What luck for rulers that men do not think.

Adolf Hitler

The average person thinks he isn't.

Larry Lorenzoni

Thoughts are not reality.

Emily Weeks

The only reason some people get lost in thought is because it is
unfamiliar territory.

Paul Fix

Thinking well is wise, planning well wiser,
doing well, wisest and best of all.

**Persian Proverb**

Creative thinking may simply mean the realisation that there is no
particular virtue in doing things the way they have always been done.

**Rudolph Flesch**

Thoughts are shadows of our feelings; always darker, emptier and
simpler.

**Friedrich Nietzsche**

You are today where your thoughts have brought you.
You will be tomorrow where your thoughts take you.

**James Alan**

Life consists of what one is thinking about all day.

**Ralph Waldo Emerson**

Don't be pushed around by the fears in your mind,
be led by the dreams in your heart.

**Roy T. Bennett**

A Tavern is a place where madness is sold by the bottle.

**Jonathan Swift**

Let go of the thoughts that don't serve you well.

**Patrick O'Leary**

Nothing limits achievement like small thinking.
Nothing expands possibilities like unleashed thinking.

**William Arthur Ward**

Stress test your thinking with the smartest people you know.

**Ray Dalio**

People calculate too much and think too little.

**Charles T. Munger**

Think for yourself and question authority.

**Timothy Leary**

You cannot think any deeper than your vocabulary will allow you to.

**George C. Fraser**

# Trust

Love all, trust few, do wrong to none.

**William Shakespeare**

It is a good maxim, to trust a person entirely or not at all.

**Henry Fielding**

Trust is the glue of life.
It's the most essential ingredient in effective communication.
It's the foundational principle that holds all relationships.

**Stephen R. Covy**

Trust but verify.

**Suzanne Massie**

Why, oh why are human beings so hard to teach, but so easy to deceive.

**Dio Chrysostom**

The trust we put in ourselves, makes us feel trust in others.

**Francois De La Rochefoucauld**

One's life would be wretched and confined if it were to miss
the candid intimacy developed by mutual trust and esteem.

**Edwin Dummer**

A feeling of distrust is always the last which a great mind acquires.

**Jean Baptiste Racine**

Never trust a man who, when left alone in a room with a tea-cosy, doesn't try it on.

**Billy Connolly**

Trust, like fine china, once broken can be repaired, but it is never quite the same.

**Mark Manson**

To them you tell your secrets, to them you resign your liberty.

**Spanish Proverb**

The best way to find out if you can trust somebody is to trust them.

**Ernest Hemingway**

Trust starts with truth and ends with truth.

**Santosh Kalwar**

Few delights can equal the mere presence of one whom we trust utterly.

**George MacDonald**

A body of men holding themselves accountable to nobody ought not to be trusted by anybody.

**Thomas Paine**

Trust is not an obsession; it's an extension of love.
When we truly love someone, we give them our heart to hold in their hands.
And when that love is returned, that very trust is balm to our souls.

**Julie Lessman**

Never be afraid to trust an unknown future to a known God.

**Corrie Ten Boom**

Consistency is the true foundation of trust.

**Roy T. Bennett**

In this age, trust is the new currency for riches.

**Bernard Kelvin Clive**

Never trust the advice of a man in difficulties.

**Aesop**

Peace and trust take years to build and seconds to shatter.

**Makogany Silverain**

Cultivating genuine self-trust is at the heart of living and loving fully.

**Tara Brach**

# Truth

Truth never hurts the teller.

**Robert Browning**

To thine own self be true.

**William Shakespeare**

The truth shall make you free.

**John 8:32**

It takes two to speak the truth, one to speak and another to hear.

**Henry David Thoreau**

The truth is on the march and nothing will stop it.

**Emile Zola**

The effort to strive for truth has to precede all other matters.

**Albert Einstein**

Truth is not beautiful, neither is it ugly.
Why should it be either? Truth is truth.

**Owen C. Middleton**

What is is; and what ain't, ain't.

**Joseph E. Granville**

God offers to every mind its choice between truth and repose.
Take which you please; you can never have both.

**R. W. Emerson**

In war, truth is the first casualty.

**Aeschylus**

The truth is always the strongest argument.

**Sophocles**

Truth is the foundation of all knowledge and the cement of all societies.

**John Dryden**

The truth is generally seen, rarely heard.

**Gracian**

All truths that are kept silent become poisonous.

**Friedrich Nietzsche**

It is the calling of great people, not so much to preach new truths, as to rescue from oblivion those old truths, which it is our wisdom to remember and our weakness to forget.

**Sydney Smith**

The language of truth is simple.

**Euripides**

Theories are private property, but truth is common stock.

**Charles Caleb Colton**

Truth has no special time of its own.
Its hour is now, always.

**Albert Schweitzer**

No matter what you believe in, it doesn't change the facts.

**Al Kersha**


The high-minded person must care more for the truth than what people think.

**Aristotle**


If 50 million people say a foolish thing, it is still a foolish thing.

**Bertrand Russell**


Truth will rise above falsehood as oil above water.

**Miguel De Cervantes**


We live in the present, we dream of the future and
we learn eternal truths from the past.

**M. M. E. Chiang Kai-Shek**


We must never throw away a bushel of truth, because it happens to contain a few grains of chaff.

**Dean Stanley**


Truth is often eclipsed, but never extinguished.

**Livy**


The spirit of truth and the spirit of freedom – they are the pillars of society.

**Henrik Ibsen**


One who seeks truth and loves it must be reckoned precious to any human society.

**Frederick The Great**

Keep true, never be ashamed of doing right;
decide on what you think is right and stick to it.

**George Eliot**

Truth is, everyone is going to hurt you;
you just gotta find the ones worth suffering for.

**Bob Marley**

# Values

Your personal core values define who you are.

**Anthony Hsieh**

Try not to become a person of success, but rather a person of value.

**Albert Einsten**

Good values are like a magnet - they attract good people.

**John Wooden**

Your core values are the deeply held beliefs that authentically describe your soul.

**John C. Maxwell**

Our value is the sum of our values.

**Joseph Batten**

Good moral values are mostly moulded from a place where love, faith and hope exist.

**Arsenid V. Manalo**

Never compromise your values.

**Stephen Maraboli**

Maturity is achieved when a person postpones immediate pleasures for long term values.

**Joshua L. Liebman**

The aim of education is the knowledge, not of facts but of values.

**William Inge**

Great people have great values and great ethics.

**Jeffrey Gitomer**

There is too much stress today on material things.
I try to teach my children not so much the value of cents, but a sense of value.

**Morris Franklin**

If you really do put a small value upon yourself, rest assured that the world will not raise your price.

**John C. Maxwell**

You have to maintain a culture of transformation and stay true to your values.

**Jeff Weiner**

With the right people, culture and values, you can accomplish great things.

**Patricia Griffith**

For me, I am driven by two main philosophies:
Know more today about the world than I did yesterday and lessen the suffering of others.
You'd be surprised how far it gets you.

**Neil de Grasse Tyson**

Tell me what you pay attention to and I will tell you who you are.

**José Ortega y Gasset**

A highly developed value system is like a compass.
It serves as a guide to you in the right direction when you are lost.

**Idowu Koyenikan**

When we cannot bear to be alone, it means we do not properly value
the only companion we will have from birth to death – ourselves.

**Eda Leshan**

Peace of mind comes when our life is in harmony with true principles
and values and in no other way.

**Stephen Covey**

Values provide perspective in the best of times and the worst.

**Charles Garfield**

Before you call yourself a Christian, Buddhist, Muslim, Hindu
or any other theology, learn to be human first.

**Shannon L. Alder**

Find people who share your values and you'll conquer the world
together.

**John Ratzenberger**

# Wisdom

To be fond of learning is near to wisdom.

**Confucius**

True wisdom lies in gathering the precious things out of each day as it goes by.

**E. S. Bouton**

A single conversation with a wise person is better than 10 years of study.

**Chinese Proverb**

Time ripens all things; no person is born wise.

**Cervantes**

The growth of wisdom may be gauged accurately by the decline of ill temper.

**Friedrich Nietzsche**

Acknowledging what you don't know is the dawning of wisdom.

**Charles Munger**

As a man grows wiser, he talks less and says more.

**Plato**

We don't receive wisdom; we must discover it for ourselves after a journey that no one can take for us or spare us.

**Marcel Proust**

It is time to turn on to an older wisdom that, while respecting material comfort and security as a basic right for all, also recognising that many of the most valuable things in life cannot be counted.

**President Michael D. Higgins**

To keep your secret is wisdom; but to expect others to keep it is folly.

**Samuel Johnson**

There is no pillow so soft as a clear conscience.

**French Proverb**

From the errors of others, a wise person corrects their own.

**Publilius Syrus**

The first step in the acquisition of wisdom is silence;
the second, listening; the third, memory;
the fourth, practice; and the fifth, teaching others.

**Solomon Ibn Gabirol**

Wisdom, compassion and courage, are the three universally recognised moral qualities of man.

**Confucius**

Nature and wisdom never are at strife.

**Plutarch**

Everything that irritates us about others can lead us to an understanding of ourselves.

**Carl Jung**

The wisdom of the wise is an uncommon degree of common sense.

**William Ralph Inge**

Wisdom is knowing when to speak your mind and when to mind your speech.

**Evangel**

The art of being wise is the art of knowing what to overlook.

**William James**

Ninety percent of all human wisdom is the ability to mind your own business.

**Robert A. Heinelein**

Wisdom is often nearer when we stoop than when we soar.

**William Wordsworth**

Wisdom is the capacity to realise what is of value in life, for oneself and others, and pursue it.

**Socrates**

Valuing the good things in life, family, friends, health and purposeful activity is one of the cornerstones of true wisdom.

**Anne Moreland**

Wisdom lies not in trying to be somebody, but in trying to help somebody.

**Lewis Howes**

We should keep our feet on the ground to signify that nothing is beneath us,
but we should also lift up our eyes to see nothing is beyond us.

**Seamus Heaney**


Those who love wisdom must be inquirers into many different things indeed.

**Heraclitus**


See everything, overlook a great deal, improve a little.

**Pope John XXIII**

#  Work

Without labour nothing prospers.

**Sophocles**

Employment is nature's physician and is essential to human happiness.

**Galen**

We work to become, not to acquire.

**Elbert Hubbard**

Find something you love to do and you'll never have to work a day in your life.

**Harvey Mackay**

Work spares us from three great evils: boredom, vice and need.

**Voltaire**

God gives every bird its food, but he does not throw it into the nest.

**J. G. Holland**

Whatever is worth doing at all, is worth doing well.

**Philip Dormer Stanhope**

The have and the have nots, can often be traced back to the dids and did nots.

**D. O'Flynn**

Small projects need more help than great ones.

**Dante Alighieri**

Keep doing the simple things better.

**John P. O'Neill**

Light is the task where many share the toil.

**Homer**

I never did a day's work in my life. It was all fun.

**Thomas Edison**

Find out what you are best at and keep pounding away at it.

**Simon Marks**

It is easier to do a job right, than to explain why you didn't.

**Martin Van Buren**

He worked like hell in the country so he could live in the city,
where he worked like hell to live in the country.

**Don Marquis**

My Grandfather told me there are two kinds of people:
those who do the work and those who take the credit.
He told me to try to be in the first group; there was less competition
there.

**Indira Gandhi**

An unpaid job is the hardest to resign from.

**T. K. Whitaker**

Behold the turtle: he only makes progress when he sticks his neck out.

**James Bryant Conant**

Of all the unhappy people in the world, the unhappiest are those who have not found something they want to do.
True happiness comes to them who do their work well, followed by a relaxing and refreshing period of rest.

**Lin Yutang**

Work is the greatest thing in the world, so we should always save some of it for tomorrow.

**Don Herold**

The future depends on what you do today.

**Mahatma Gandhi**

They are happy whose natures sort with their vocations.

**Francis Bacon**

Work for a cause, not for applause.

**Grace Lichtenstein**

Let everyone practice the art they know best.

**Cicero**

For me, hard work represents the supreme luxury of life.

**Albert M. Greenfield**

If you want to leave your footprints on the sands of time, be sure you're wearing work shoes.

**Italian Proverb**

A people, secure in their jobs, taking pride in their work and sure of just recognition will help our society grow to new heights.

**James F. Lincoln**

People forget how fast you did a job, but they remember how well you did it.

**Howard W. Newton**

When your life moves from survival to service, your life blossoms.

**Daniel Sullivan**

# Worry

Worry is interest paid on trouble before it becomes due.

**William Ralph Inge**

Worrying is like sitting in a rocking chair:
it gives you something to do, but it never gets you anywhere.

**Emma Bombeck**

Shut the iron doors on the past and the future.
Live in day tight compartments.

**Dale Carnegie**

As a cure for worrying, work is better than whiskey.

**Thomas A. Edison**

You will break the worry habit, the day you decide you can meet
and master the worst that can happen to you.

**Arnold Glasow**

Everything you ever wanted, is on the other side of fear.

**George Adair**

Worry pretends to be necessary, but it serves no useful purpose.

**Eckhart Tolle**

All men's miseries derive from not being able to sit in a quiet room
alone.

**Blaise Pascal**

There is many a pessimist who got that way by financing an optimist.

**Anonymous**

Let our advance worrying, become advanced thinking and planning.

**Winston Churchill**

It's not time to worry yet.

**Harper Lee**

Sorrow looks back, worry looks around, faith looks up.

**Ralph Waldo Emerson**

If you have fear of some pain or suffering, you should examine whether there is anything you can do about it.
If you can, there is no need to worry about it;
if you cannot do anything, then there is also no need to worry.

**Dalai Lama**

I am an old man and have known a great many troubles, but most of them never happened.

**Mark Twain**

Worry gives a small thing a big shadow.

**Swedish Proverb**

Worry is a misuse of imagination.

**Daniel Zadra**

The scariest events are usually not the most important.

**Louis-Vincent Gave**

We would worry less if we praised more. Thanksgiving is the enemy of discontent.

**Harry A. Ironside**

The elimination diet:
Remove anger, regret, resentment, guilt, blame and worry.
Then watch your health and life improve.

**Charles F. Glassman**

It ain't no use putting up your umbrella till it rains.

**Alice Caldwell Rice**

Pain is inevitable, suffering is optional.

**Dalai Lama**

Fear knocked, faith answered – nobody was there.

**Martin Luther King Jr.**

# ❧ Youth ❧

Youth is a young life plus curiosity minus understanding.

**Anthony Brooks**

A child's life is like a piece of paper on which every passerby
leaves a mark.

**Chinese Proverb**

Youth is a circumstance you can't do anything about.
The trick is to grow up without getting old.

**Frank Lloyd Wright**

You are only young once, but you can be immature forever.

**John P. Grier**

The old believe everything;
the middle-aged suspect everything;
the young know everything.

**Oscar Wilde**

Youth is wholly experimental.

**Robert Louis Stevenson**

Youth and beauty fade; character endures forever.

**Gayland Anderson**

To stay youthful, stay useful.

**John Keats**

Whom the Gods love die young, no matter how long they live.

**Elbert Hubbard**

During the first period of one's life, the greatest danger is: not to take the risk.

**Soren Kierkegaard**

A child becomes an adult when they realise they have a right
not only to be right but also to be wrong.

**Thomas Szasz**

To a supercilious youth who said he, "simply couldn't bear fools".
"How odd, your Mother could apparently".

**Dorothy Parker**

Girls, we love for what they are, young men for what they
promise to be.

**Johann Wolfgang Von Goethe**

This is a youth-oriented society and the joke is on them because,
youth is a disease from which we all recover.

**Dorothy Fuldheim**

Be on alert to recognise your prime at whatever time of your life it
may occur.

**Muriel Spark**

Youth is a gift of nature, but age is work of art.

**Stanislaw Jerzy Lec**

The foundation of every state is the education of its youth.

**Diogenes**

In youth we learn, in age we understand.

**Marie Von Ebner-Eschenbach**

Forty is the old age of youth; fifty is the youth of old age.

**Victor Hugo**

Youth is happy because it has the ability to see beauty.
Anyone who keeps the ability to see beauty never grows old.

**Franz Kafka**

Ageing is not lost youth, but a new stage of opportunity and strength.

**Elizabeth Friedan**

Take risks in your life. If you win, you may lead.
If you lose, you may guide.

**Swami Vivekananda**

# Acknowledgements

"Alone we can do little, together we can do much" said Helen Keller, author and political activist who lost her sight and hearing at 19 months old.

So it is with the publication of this book that I would sincerely like to acknowledge the contribution of many people who helped bring it to fruition.

Firstly, I would like to thank all the people quoted in this book, living and dead, for their wisdom and for taking the time to have their quotations available for all of us to benefit from.

I would like to thank my good friend, Mark Walsh for suggesting some of the chapters for the book, chapters I would have overlooked.

To our three daughters, Sarah, Amy, Jenny and our son-in-law Brendan for also looking at the chapters and quotations to see if they would resonate with the next generation.

To my sister Margaret McGovern for the many hours of typing and retyping edited versions, until we were happy with the finished article.

To our publisher, Orla Kelly and her team for their guidance, support and expertise in bringing this book to reality.

To my wonderful wife Valerie, whose patience and support made this book possible and who makes every day of our journey a fulfilling and meaningful adventure.

Last, but not least to you the reader. Thank you for taking the time to read this book and I hope it serves you well.

# About the Author

Tadhg McCarthy is Managing Director of McCarthy Investment Services Limited, a company he founded in Cork, Ireland in 1981.

He holds a Diploma in Social Studies from University Cork and he also holds a Higher Diploma in Coaching Psychology also from the same University.

One of his passions is travel and having travelled across the world over the past 40 years, the quotations in this book are from many different countries and cultures.

Tadhg is a native of Midleton, Co Cork Ireland and still lives there with his wife Valerie, 3 daughters, 2 dogs and a cat.